HOW TO PLAY GUITAR

THE BASICS & BEYOND

CHORDS, SCALES, TUNES & TIPS

By the Editors of

GuitarPlayer®

Backbeat Books

San Francisco

Published by Backbeat Books
600 Harrison Street, San Francisco, CA 94107
www.backbeatbooks.com
E-mail: books@musicplayer.com
An imprint of Music Player Network
United Entertainment Media, Inc.
Publishers of *Guitar Player, Bass Player,* and *Keyboard* magazines

Distributed to the book trade in the U.S. and Canada by
Publishers Group West, 1700 Fourth Street, Berkeley, CA 94710

Distributed to the music trade in the U.S. and Canada by
Hal Leonard Publishing, P.O. Box 13819, Milwaukee, WI 53213

ISBN 0-87930-661-0

Editor: Richard Johnston and Jesse Gress
Cover Design: Richard Leeds
Cover Photo: Ken Settle
Design: Samuel Miranda and Brad Greene

Printed in the United States of America
01 02 03 04 05   5 4 3 2 1

CONTENTS

INTRODUCTION TO THE SECOND EDITION

Imagine walking into a music store that's stocked wall to wall and floor to ceiling with gleaming new guitars of every make, model, color, and size, acoustic and electric—every sort of axe you've ever dreamed about or seen your heroes playing. Then imagine the store owner saying, "Go ahead; take a few—whichever ones you want."

The problem would be, of course, deciding which ones *not* to take.

When we were publishing the first *How To Play* issues at *Guitar Player* way back in the mid '90s, the hardest task of assembling any given issue was honing down the material at hand. After all, we were tapping into an unparalleled resource—a quarter-century's worth of *Guitar Player* lessons from a galaxy of great players and teachers in most every style of music.

We were pleased with the results, even more so when the series grew into a bimonthly publication, and then when our book division turned the best of our efforts into a softcover edition. *How To Play Guitar* went on to become one of their best-selling titles.

For this new edition, Backbeat Books author and long-time *Guitar Player* music editor Jesse Gress has polished and expanded the lessons and added a chapter of his own. In addition, we've enlisted prominent technical writer Terry Buddingh to update the crucial advice on buying an instrument and amplifier. What hasn't changed is the treasury of information on picking and strumming, chords and scales, and music in general—enough to get you started on the basics and keep you busy for quite a while. You can also listen to twelve of the lessons on the TrueFire.com/Notes On Call CD that's included inside the back cover.

Whether you're an adult learner or a youngster starting out, the lessons in this new edition of *How To Play Guitar* will save you time—and money—and be a reference you can return to again and again. So get started—it's your turn to make music.

—*Richard Johnston*

NOTATIONAL SYMBOLS

T he following symbols are used in *How To Play Guitar* to notate fingerings, techniques, and effects commonly used in guitar music. Certain symbols are found in either the tablature or the standard notation only, not both. For clarity, consult both systems.

4 : Left-hand fingering is designated by small Arabic numerals near note heads (1=first finger, 2=middle finger, 3=third finger, 4=little finger, t=thumb).

p : Right-hand fingering designated by letters (p=thumb, i=first finger, m=middle finger, a=third finger, c=little finger).

② : A circled number (1-6) indicates the string on which a note is to be played.

⊓ : Pick downstroke.

V : Pick upstroke.

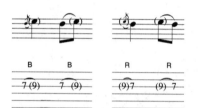

Bend: Play the first note and bend to the pitch of the equivalent fret position shown in parentheses.

Reverse Bend: Prebend the note to the specified pitch/fret position shown in parentheses. Play, then release to indicated pitch/fret.

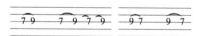

Hammer-on: From lower to higher note(s). Individual notes may also be hammered.

Pull-off: From higher to lower note(s).

Slide: Play first note and slide up or down to the next pitch. If the notes are tied, pick only the first. If no tie is present, pick both.

Finger vibrato.

Bar vibrato.

Bar dips, dives, and bends: Numerals and fractions indicate distance of bar bends in half-steps.

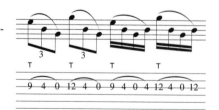

Natural harmonics. Artificial harmonics.

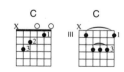

Pick-hand tapping: Notes are hammered with a pick-hand finger, usually followed by additional hammer-ons and pull-offs.

even gliss

A slide symbol before or after a single note indicates a slide to or from an undetermined pitch.

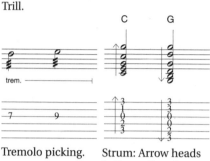

Trill.

trem.

Tremolo picking.

Strum: Arrow heads indicate direction.

How Tablature Works

The horizontal lines represent the guitar's strings, the top line standing for the high *E*. The numbers designate the frets to be played. For instance, a 2 positioned on the first line would mean play the 2nd fret on the first string (0 indicates an open string). Time values are indicated on the standard notation staff seen directly above the tablature. Special symbols and instructions appear between the standard and tablature staves.

Chord Diagrams

In all *How To Play Guitar* chord diagrams, vertical lines represent the strings, and horizontal lines represent the frets. The following symbols are used:

▬▬▬ Nut; indicates first position.

X   Muted string, or string not played.

○   Open string.

⌒   Barre (partial or full).

●   Placement of left-hand fingers.

III Roman numerals indicate the fret at which a chord is located.

Arabic numerals indicate left-hand fingering.

TRACK 2

Stringing & Tuning

BY JOHNNY SMITH

More and more players today depend on electronic tuners, and unfortunately, they are bypassing the chance to develop their ability to hear the difference between good and bad intonation. I'm not dead set against electronic tuners, but guitarists should learn how to tune by ear.

There's a sitcom that plays out often at our store. A customer lays a fine guitar on the counter and informs me that the frets are in the

John Mooney photo by Brian Blauser

wrong place. The first-position *C* chord sounds in tune, but the seventh-position *E* major chord is all out of whack. The customer is right. But chances are, it isn't because of the frets. Instead, it's a classic case of the guitar not being tuned properly.

Another frequent complaint is that "the keys are slipping." But the chance of even the cheapest tuners slipping is extremely remote. The problem invariably turns out to be the way the strings were put on—there are open loops around the key posts, not enough turns around them to lock the strings, or a lack of understanding of the tuners themselves. If there are open loops around the post, or if an unwrapped (plain) string isn't wrapped around the post enough times, a little tug on the string will usually cause it to loosen like a wet noodle.

TRACK 1

PUTTING ON STRINGS

The variations in stringing methods are a never-ending source of amazement and amusement. Some folks feel that you have to tie knots in the strings around the posts. Others think that you have to run the strings through the post hole as many times as the string's diameter allows, while still others believe that you should use every inch of the string, ending up with an unstable blob of wire wrapped around the post. But excess windings can cause the string to twist, and if twisted enough, the string may vibrate inconsistently and produce a false pitch. The idea is to string in a way that facilitates installation and changing. I often have to waste a half-hour at the workbench just removing strings that were put on wrong. Customers are lucky I don't charge the same hourly rate as their plumber.

EX. 1

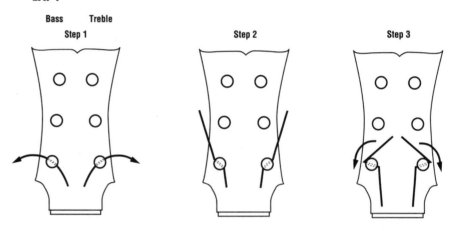

One of the best methods of stringing is shown in **Ex. 1**. After putting it through the post hole, bend the string sharply to lock it to the post right from the start. You should have approximately three turns for each wrapped string, and about twice as many on the unwrapped strings. This, plus a generous amount of stretching, results in a very stable string. Winding the loose string toward the bottom of the post greatly reduces leverage and torque on the post, therefore reducing gear wear.

Take the time to look at the pin block of a piano. The makers of even the cheapest pianos realize one thing above all else: The strings have to be put on correctly, or those manufacturers will be out of business—period. If the strings aren't correctly installed, there is no way the instrument will hold a tuning long enough to get it off of the showroom floor. For the concerned player, the guitar is the same. **Ex. 2** shows tidy lower-string winding; **Ex. 3** shows a sloppy job.

EX. 2

EX. 3

photos by Nora Sturges

GETTING IN TUNE

Tuning well is like playing well—it takes practice and time. And good intonation is essential for good musicianship. A few out-of-tune strings can destroy the beauty of the best piano in the world. And one out-of-tune guitar can foul up the sound of an entire band.

Through the years, I have watched really fine players frequently reach up and tweak one key and then another while playing. The chances of their guitars being in tune at any one time are remote, to say the least. Their single-line melodies were not offensive, but when it came time to sustain even a major chord, it was not acceptable.

Accepting the fact that humans vary from day to day, we need a tuning system that works on bad days as well as good, that works when we have to tune while other instruments are playing in the background, or when we have a head cold. On some days everything you play comes out perfect. Then, the very next day, the opposite is true—everything sounds awful. The same holds true for tuning.

With some practice and application, the following method of tuning should work well—or at least get you into the ballpark—even under the most adverse conditions. Although this sequence can be accomplished quickly, you must be patient and take your time when you're starting out. Let the notes sustain, and listen carefully for differences in pitch between each set of two strings.

Though there are a few lucky people with perfect intonation, for the rest of us, the ability to tune—like the ability to play the instrument—can be developed.

What does it take to develop the ability to tune and set intonation? First, you must be able to hear the difference between two tones. Try this exercise: Tune the fretted *E* at the 5th fret of the second string to the same pitch as the open high *E* string. Pick the two strings simultaneously. If both strings are at the same pitch, they will sound like one string, with no vibrato. If there is a slight difference in pitch, there will be a slow vibrato, or "beat." As the difference between pitches increases, the vibrato's speed also increases. Listening for and being able to recognize that pulse is the secret to fine-tuning the guitar. For the wave to be heard and recognized, the two strings must be allowed to sustain as long as possible, because if the pitch of the strings is very close—but not quite exact—it takes time for the wave to build in intensity.

ALWAYS TUNE "UP"

Some players have the bad habit of tuning the string too high and then lowering the pitch and leaving the key as is. This leaves just enough space—perhaps only thousandths of an inch—left in the tuning gear to allow the string to go flat when picked. The answer? Always tune at least a half-step *below* the desired pitch: Stretch the string to make sure there is no slack left in the gear, and then tune up to the correct pitch. You can prove the effectiveness of this very easily by tuning the high *E* string sharp (too high), and then backing off until the pitch is the same as the *E* at the 5th fret on the *B* string. Next give a firm tug on the first string and listen to how flat (low) it is. Now reverse the procedure: Tune the *E* string sharp and compare its pitch with the fretted *E* on the second string. Then tune the *E* string about a half-step lower than the fingered *E*, stretch the string firmly, and tune up to the desired pitch. If you tug on the string, you'll notice how much better it stays in tune. The bottom line? Always tune *up* to pitch.

THE BASICS

Every guitarist should own an electronic tuner for basic tuning, but as we've noted, it's not adequate to tune using only those devices. As you're starting out, use the method shown in **Ex. 4**. The open *E* can be tuned initially by comparing

FIG. 4

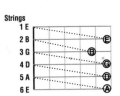

it with an *E* below middle *C* on a piano, or it can be tuned using your electronic tuner. Next, fret on the low *E* string as shown in the chart, comparing that note with the sound of the adjacent open string. Adjust the open string so the intonation matches. Then fret on the *A* string and adjust the open *D* string, etc. For fine-tuning see page 12.

STRING GAUGES

String gauges can greatly affect intonation. For solidbody guitars using sets with an unwrapped *G* string, I have found that the following gauges give the best results when setting up intonation: .010, .013, .017, .026, .036, and .046. It has been my experience that extra-light and super-light strings are all but impossible to set up with good intonation.

For acoustic-body electrics and straight acoustic guitars, most players correctly use sets with wrapped *G* strings, which greatly minimize intonation problems. Plain third strings are often the main source of faulty intonation. These have a tendency to sound sharp, and if they are too light, bridge saddle adjustment cannot compensate for them. On a well-adjusted bridge, the saddle insert for a plain *G* string is invariably located closer to the rear of the bridge than are the other inserts. This is why I do not recommend using plain thirds on acoustic archtop and flat-top guitars with slanted bridge saddles that cannot be adjusted for individual strings.

On archtop and flat-top acoustics, the second string can also cause an intonation problem. If the *B* string is too heavy, it reacts in the same way as the plain third—it has a tendency to go sharp in the upper register. Back in the days of the big band rhythm guitar, very heavy strings were the norm. As a result, the bridge saddles had to be notched out to the rear under the second string to improve intonation. But with the string gauges now used on most hollowbody guitars, a notched-out bridge saddle would cause the second string to fret flat in the upper register. Most manufacturers now use an un-notched, slanted bridge saddle that gives excellent intonation with strings of or near these gauges: .012, .016, .024 (wound), .032, .042, and .054.

For guitars such as classical and folk models that have fixed bridges, different gauges are usually the only solution to intonation problems. Some classical-guitar builders cut an offset to the rear under the third string to compensate for the inherent sharp qualities of the unwrapped nylon third string.

SETTING INTONATION

If you want to play in tune, good setup is a must. And after you start developing your "ear"—your ability to hear pitches—you can do your own setup. This involves adjusting the bridge to get the string in tune along most of its length. The technique is no deep, dark secret; setting intonation can be done adequately by most players without the use of an electronic tuner or gifted musical ears. I will always remember the beautiful, sparkling sound of the pianos when I was doing studio work in New York City. Even to this day, most of the best piano tuners I know carry their tuning kits in one coat pocket: a tuning fork, a strip of felt, a rubber wedge, and a tuning hammer. Through years of experience, they have trained their ears to be able to set up a tempered scale that's the most accurate for a particular instrument. I believe the same is true for guitars: Each one is a little different in its acoustic response—even the solidbodies.

THE FIRST STRING

Some people set the bridge or insert by aligning the pitch of the fretted *E* at the 12th fret to the harmonic *E* at that fret. This alone is all right, but if you really want to nail it down, adjust the first string so the fingered *B* at the 19th fret has the same pitch as the harmonic *B* at the 19th fret; now you can be sure that the bridge/insert for the first string is correct. Rule: If the fretted note is sharp compared with the harmonic, move the bridge/insert back, increasing the string length. If the fretted note is flat compared with the harmonic, move the bridge/insert forward, decreasing the string length. For archtop guitars with movable bridges and slanted saddles, this is the only bridge adjustment you should make. If intonation problems still exist after these adjustments, you may have to try different string gauges. The base of the bridge should not be canted (angled).

Using harmonics to tune or adjust the intonation of your guitar would be all right if you played only harmonics all the time. This is not the way it is, and the only realistic method is to set the intonation to fretted notes up the neck—which is the way you play, for the most part.

THE OTHER STRINGS

Start by tuning the second string so the pitch of the fretted *E* (5th fret) matches the open first string **(Ex. 5)**. Let the notes sustain while you are doing this. Then use the sequence in **Ex. 6** to set the intonation for the remaining five strings. (Note that the fingered notes in each diagram spell out a major chord: root, third, fifth, root.) The sequence for the third string is especially helpful for setting an unwrapped *G* string's intonation.

A word of advice: At the beginning of each sequence, be exacting when tuning the first fretted note to the open string. If the pitch of each pair of strings is not exactly the same, the rest of the sequence will be useless. The sequence beginning with the open third string works equally well for the electric bass, even though the pitches are one octave lower.

EX. 5

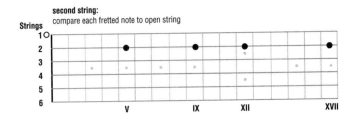

EX. 6

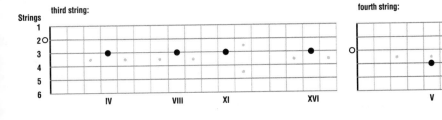

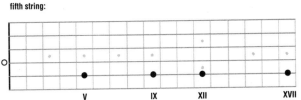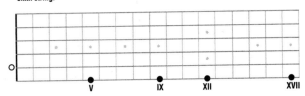

FINE-TUNING

As you grow more comfortable with your ability to hear pitches, learn to use this method to fine-tune your guitar. Use the basic tuning method first so that the neck tension won't change dramatically when you fine-tune.

Step 1: Make sure the high *E* string (first string) is tuned to the correct pitch.

Step 2: Tune the fretted *E* (5th fret, *B* string) to the open first-string *E*.

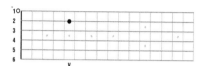

You can cross-check by comparing the fretted note to a harmonic. To produce a harmonic, lightly touch—don't depress—the *B* string at the 12th fret. You should hear a chime-like tone. Compare that note to the fretted *B* at the 7th fret on the first string. Remember to let the strings sustain and listen carefully for "beating." Adjust the *B* string. When you've made the beat stop, the string is in tune.

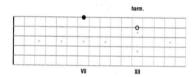

Step 3: Because of the characteristics of unwrapped third strings, this method works on nylon as well as metal strings. Tune the fretted *E* (9th fret, *G* string) to the open high *E* string.

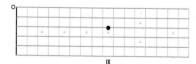

Cross-check by comparing the harmonic at the 12th fret of the *G* string with the fretted *G* (3rd fret, high *E* string).

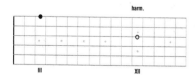

Step 4: Tune the fretted *B* (9th fret, fourth string) to the open *B* string.

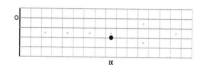

Cross-check by comparing the harmonic at the 12th fret on the *D* string to the fretted *D* (3rd fret, *B* string).

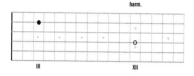

Step 5: Tune the fretted *G* (10th fret, *A* string) to the open *G*.

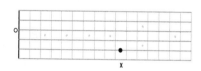

Cross-check by comparing the harmonic at the 12th fret on the *A* string with the fretted *A* (2nd fret, *G* string).

Step 6: Tune the fretted *D* (10th fret, low *E* string) to the open *D* string.

Cross-check by comparing the harmonic at the 12th fret on the low *E* string with the fretted *E* (2nd fret, *D* string).

Use the following sequence for checking intonation quickly during performances: ■

B string

G string

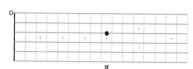

D string

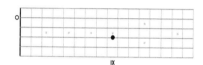

A string

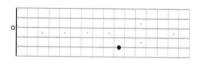

Low *E* string

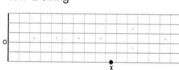

How to Read Music

BY TOM DARTER

For some strange reason, reading music is a mystery to many musicians. It is not unusual for an adult with a degree in physics to walk into a studio to sign up for guitar lessons, only to say, "I'll take lessons if I don't have to learn to read music." This same person might be a bit embarrassed to learn the guitar teacher has probably taught several hundred second- and third-graders to read simple melodies in two or three lessons.

Anyone who is willing to memorize a few basics, and practice consistently, can learn to read music. Once you have learned, you can get rusty with inactivity, but you'll never forget how to read notes.

Jacques Stotzem photo courtesy of The Martin Guitar Company

THE STAFF

The staff consists of five lines and four spaces (**Ex. 1**). The lines have names that are easy to learn by memorizing the following sentence: **E**very **G**ood **B**oy **D**oes **F**ine (**Ex. 2**). The spaces also have names, which spell the word **FACE** (**Ex. 3**).

EX. 1

EX. 2

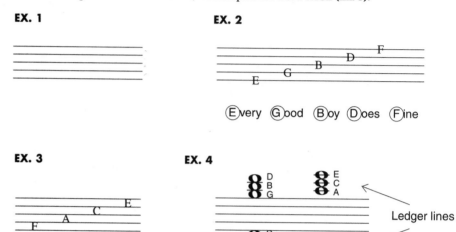

(E)very (G)ood (B)oy (D)oes (F)ine

EX. 3

EX. 4

F - A - C - E

Ledger lines

LEDGER NOTES

Sometimes notes are written above or below the staff with the use of ledger lines, as shown in **Ex. 4**. The guitar student must become familiar with the notes *above* and *below* the staff well as those *on* the staff. Speed in naming the notes in any order is important. The exercises in **Ex. 5** will help you learn the names of the notes. Write the name of each on the space below it. Buy some manuscript paper from your local music store and make up your own exercises.

EX. 5

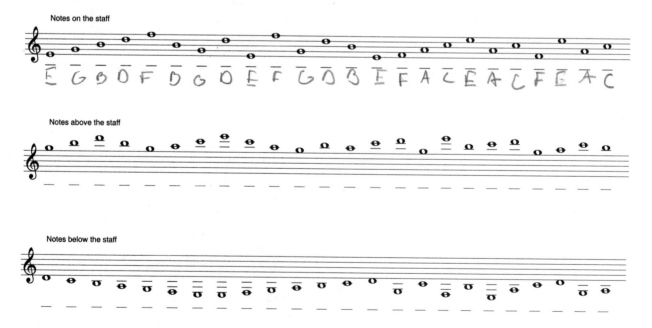

THE G CLEF

The notation explained thus far is all written in the *G* (or treble) clef, which is the clef used for guitar. The *G* clef symbol in **Ex. 6** circles the second line, establishing it as *G*.

EX. 6

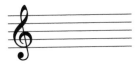

NOTES

Concentrate on rapidly naming the notes on and below the staff. Your success in reading music depends on this! **Ex. 7** shows where some of these notes are found on the guitar. **Caution:** Do not confuse the five lines of the staff with the six strings on the guitar or the six lines of a tablature staff.

EX. 7
1st string:

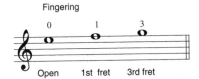

Play each note until you have a mental picture of it. Say the names aloud. Now, try playing the notes in **Ex. 8**.

EX. 8

Memorize the notes on strings two through six, as shown in **Ex. 9**.

EX. 9

2nd string:

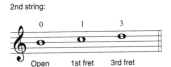

Exercise on 2nd string:

3rd string:

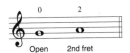

Exercise on 2nd and 3rd strings:

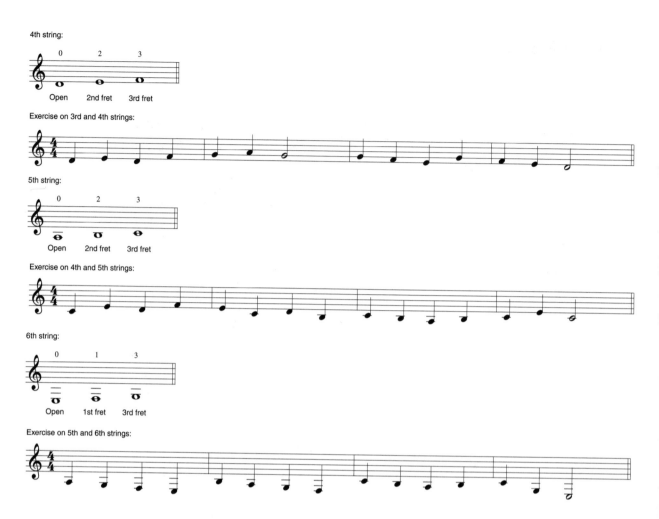

4th string:

Open 2nd fret 3rd fret

Exercise on 3rd and 4th strings:

5th string:

Open 2nd fret 3rd fret

Exercise on 4th and 5th strings:

6th string:

Open 1st fret 3rd fret

Exercise on 5th and 6th strings:

So that the player knows how long to hold a note before proceeding to the next, each type of note is assigned a value. In popular time signatures such as 4/4, 3/4, and 2/4, the values are assigned as shown in **Ex. 10**.

Many of the musical examples in *How To Play Guitar* are in a particular key. That is, they use one of the major or minor scales for their structure. So if a piece is based on the *C* major scale, it is said to be in the key of *C* major. The notes of that key are *C-D-E-F-G-A-B-C*.

When a piece of music is based on a scale that starts on a note other than *C*, however, sharps (♯) or flats (♭) must be added to preserve the correct relationship (interval) between notes, which in a major key is whole-step (two frets), whole-step, half-step (one fret), whole-step, whole-step, whole-step, half-step.

Each key has its own *key signature*, which indicates which notes are sharp (raised a half-step) or flat (lowered a half-step) for that key. For example, the key signature for the key of *D* is two sharps. This means that whenever the notes *F* and *C* appear in the music, they should be automatically raised a half-step.

EX. 10

Whole-note	Half-note	Quarter-note	Eighth-note	Dotted-half
4 counts	2 counts	1 count	1/2 count	3 counts

EX. 11
CIRCLE OF 5ths

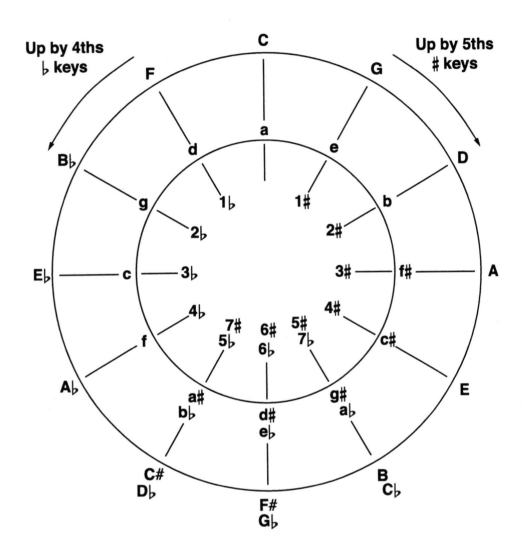

The circle of 5ths (**Ex. 11**) provides a straightforward graphic display of the patterns and relationships among keys, and understanding the circle will help guitarists see the relationships between the chords and scales they play.

The major keys that use sharps in their key signatures are found by moving around the circle in a clockwise direction beginning from *C* at the top, while the major keys that use flats are found by moving counterclockwise around the circle from *C*. The sharp keys are related by ascending perfect fifths (as the number of sharps increases), while the flat keys are related by descending perfect fifths (as the number of flats increases), and the circle shows these relationships.

The relative minor keys are displayed in the same way on the inner circle of 5ths diagram. (A major key and its relative minor share the same key signature.) To find the relative minor of a particular major key, just move along the radial line to the inner circle. Likewise, to find the relative major of a particular minor key, move along the radial line to the outer circle. The number of sharps or flats in the key signature of each key is shown in the center of the circle, at the end of each connecting radial line.

It's easy to find parallel keys and their signatures on the circle, too. (A major key and its parallel minor both start on the same note, but their key signatures are different.) To find the parallel minor of a particular major key, just move three positions around the circle in a counterclockwise direction, and look to the inner circle. To find the parallel major of a particular minor key, move three positions clockwise around the circle, and look to the outer circle.

When you need to refresh your memory on the order of appearance of sharps or flats in the basic key signatures, the circle can help. Notice that the seven basic note names *(C, D, E, F, G, A, B)* are shown in a row on the outer circle of the diagram. If you begin at *F* and move around the circle clockwise (the sharp direction), you will find the order of appearance of the sharps in the sharp key signatures *(F-C-G-D-A-E-B)*. If you begin at the other end with *B* and move around the circle counterclockwise (the flat direction), you will find the order of appearance of the flats in the flat key signatures *(B-E-A-D-G-C-F)*.

At the bottom of the diagram, you will notice that certain of the sharp and flat keys overlap. For instance, the key of *F♯* major (six sharps) occupies the same position as the key of *G♭* major (six flats). You will also notice that if you play the scale of *F♯* major on the guitar, followed by the scale of *G♭* major, you will be playing the same notes. The notes *F♯* and *G♭* are called *enharmonic equivalents*, and in our scale system, based on *equal temperament*, they sound exactly the same. It follows that the scales built up from *G♭* and *F♯* would also be enharmonically equivalent.

Now that we've covered the basic relationships shown in the circle, let's look at the reason for putting all of this information in a circle. If you play the indicated key notes around the circle in either direction, you will find an uninterrupted chain of perfect fifths that always returns to its own starting place. This continuous cycle (often referred to as the cycle of 5ths), besides showing the overall relationship of the major keys, is useful in understanding the structure of many of the chord progressions you will be playing. ■

Getting Around the Fretboard

BY JOHN CARLINI

Jennifer Batten photo by Lisa Sharken

With your guitar you will discover an exception to the phrase "familiarity breeds contempt." The more you know your fretboard, the more music you'll be able to play, and the more your affection for the instrument will grow. When you look at those 20-odd frets and six strings, though, the thought of making any kind of sense at all of the instrument may seem like a daunting task at best. The following information will help you unlock the secrets of the fretboard, over time. Fretboard mastery does not come overnight; use this information as you would a city map, referring to it as you discover new areas you'd like to explore.

First, I'd like to discuss position. William Leavitt, one of my teachers at the Berklee School of Music in Boston, explained position this way: "Position may be defined simply by which fret the index finger is playing." **Ex. 1** (next page) illustrates the second position, indicated by the Roman numeral beneath the fretboard diagram. In the second position, the index finger (1) frets any note on the 2nd fret; the middle finger (2) frets any note on the 3rd fret; the ring finger (3) frets any note on the 4th fret; and the pinky (4) frets any note on the 5th fret.

EX. 1

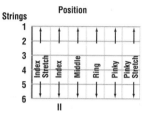

Before I discuss the stretches to other frets, I'd like to interject a few thoughts on left-hand positioning. It is very important to hold the guitar neck properly with your left hand in order to fully utilize the position concept. Make sure that your left-hand thumb is near the center of the back of the neck and that your wrist is arched downward and outward from the instrument—as though you had an imaginary golf ball in the palm of your hand.

Let your four fingers hover directly over their respective frets in the second position. With this technique, the only energy and motion required to fret a note is to push straight down with your fingers, applying a vise-like pressure with fingers and thumb. This might seem uncomfortable at first, but with consistent practice you will develop additional strength in your left hand and fingers.

With your hand properly situated in the second position, you can stretch your first finger back to play the notes on the 1st fret. Similarly, the fourth finger can stretch to play the notes on the 6th fret. Be sure to keep your left hand from moving out of position—you must maintain your positional control. This six-fret span lets you play any chord, scale, or arpeggio in one position. Or, to put it another way, any of the 12 keys can be played in this one position, and any one key can be played in all 12 positions.

Now, let's examine a *C* major scale in the second position (**Ex. 2**). Strictly speaking, the scale starts on the fifth string, at the 3rd fret (*C*), and progresses up to the third string, 5th fret (*C*, an octave higher). But from this position, you can play parts of the scale that lie in other octaves. If you continue up the scale from that third-string *C*, you can go as high as *A* on the first string. If you continue down the scale from the fifth-string *C*, you can get as low as *F* on the sixth string.

All that from the same position! In other words, Ex. 2 shows all the notes of the

EX. 2

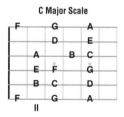

C major scale that are available in the second position. Keep your eyes on the fretboard diagram. As you watch, play the scale from *C* on the fifth string to *C* on the third string, then from low *F* to high *A*. Remember to stay in position. Stretch your index finger back to play the *F* notes on the sixth and first strings. Stretch the fourth finger up to play the *A* notes on the sixth and first strings.

After you can follow the fretboard diagram, try reading the same exercise from the notation and tablature in **Ex. 3**. (Numbers preceding notes indicate fingers; numbers on tablature strings indicate fret numbers. See the guide to notational symbols on page 6 for a detailed explanation of tablature.)

EX. 3

Experiment. Explore. Try recording a rhythm-guitar part using a *C* major chord, and then play it back while you watch the written material and improvise melodically. Use the notes of the *C* scale in any order or combination. After a while, stop watching the diagram and mentally visualize the fretboard patterns. As you gain confidence, and as your left-hand technique becomes smoother, let go of the idea that you are practicing an exercise. Allow a musical flow to develop.

As previously mentioned, one of the remarkable possibilities that opens up to you through a solid foundation in position playing is that of being able to play any major scale from any given position. In **Ex. 4** you'll find all 12 major scales with their extended ranges, all in the second position.

EX. 4

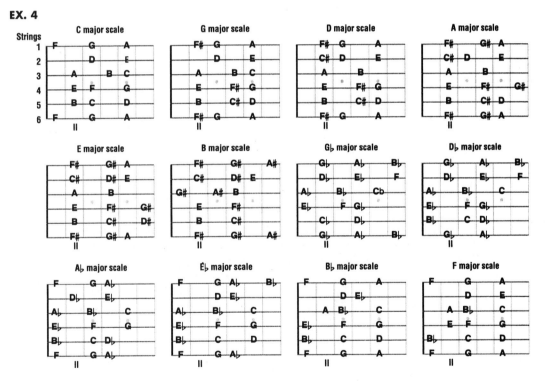

As you play each scale, be very careful to stay oriented to your 2nd-fret reference point. When stretching for the 1st fret or the 6th fret, do not lose your left-hand position. Play each scale starting on the root (tonic note) as you did with Ex. 2. Play up the scale to the octave root (eighth tone) and go back down again so that you get the sound of the key in your musical ear. Then play the entire range of each scale.

Make a rhythm guitar tape of the major chords, in any combination or sequence, and shift from scale to scale as the chords change. Notice that there are 12 fingerings, one for each major scale. Once you get familiar with these fingerings you will be able to play any major scale in any position. Remember, practicing scales is merely performing a series of exercises through which you acquire facility and technique so that you can create music.

Each major scale contains six other scales, or modes, whose names come to us from the music theory of ancient Greece. Actually, the original Greek name for the major scale is the Ionian mode. Let's take another look at the second-position *C* major scale/Ionian mode (**Ex. 5**).

EX. 5

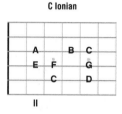

C Ionian

First, play the scale from the fifth-string *C* to the third-string *C*. The characteristic chord sound of the *C* Ionian mode is *Cmaj7*. That comes from playing the root, third, fifth, and seventh steps of the scale (*C*, *E*, *G*, and *B*). Now play those notes and the octave third-string *C*. Then, play those notes back down again (*C*, *B*, *G*, *E*, and low *C*).

Playing only the chord tones in succession is called an *arpeggio*. **Ex. 6** is a diagram of the *Cmaj7* arpeggio. To play from the third-string *C* to the second-string *E* requires that you flatten out the first joint of your fourth finger, and roll it across the 5th fret as you work those notes (*G*, *C*, and *E*). This is not an easy technique, but with a little daily practice, you can do it.

EX. 6

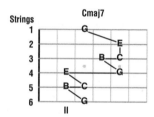

Cmaj7

Practice this arpeggio. Use the *C* major chord track you taped again for the arpeggio practice. As always, explore and experiment. Follow the diagonal line as you watch the diagram, and play any of the notes in any order.

Ex. 7 offers diagrams of all 12 major seventh arpeggios, all in the second position. You can memorize and practice these arpeggios in any order. Compare each major seventh arpeggio to its parent major scale, and notice that the arpeggio always consists of the root, third, fifth, and seventh steps of the major scale.

Record a rhythm track of each major seventh chord, four measures in slow 4/4 time. Then play it back and practice the arpeggios as you listen to the tape. You should then be able to develop many original exercises.

You might notice that some of these arpeggios are easier to play than are others. For example, the *Gmaj7* arpeggio in the second position does not require any stretches. But the *D♭maj7* arpeggio requires both first- and fourth-finger stretches, and presents you with some finger gymnastics, especially on the first three strings. What kind of gymnastics? Just maintain your position as you play the arpeggio and you'll see what I mean!

Why should you play a *D♭maj7* arpeggio in the second position anyway? Why not simply slide down to the first position, where it frets more comfortably? Because this discipline trains your hand and fingers to negotiate very unusual and difficult fingerings.

EX. 7

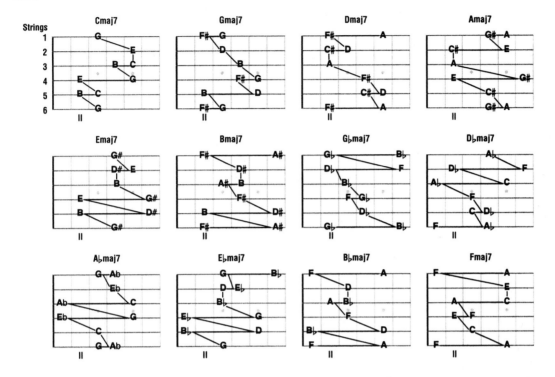

Now, here's the surprise in this Crackerjacks box: By gaining mastery in one position, you are really gaining the same facility in all positions. You develop a certain feel for the way the fretboard works, as your ear develops along with your hands and fingers. The work will pay off when you perform, and you will be able to tap this new facility right on the spot.

SCALES FOR SOLOING

Position playing can unlock a virtually limitless combination of guitar lead patterns in any key. You've found that you can play in all 12 keys in any single position. And you found that the inverse is also true: You can play in any one key in each of the 12 positions.

But most players tend to operate from preconceived ideas about what area of the fretboard works best in a given situation. For example, suppose you want to play a bluesy-sounding lick in the key of *G*. Most guitarists would head straight for the third position and dig into tried and true *G* blues turf using the *G* pentatonic minor scale. (**Ex. 8**).

EX. 8

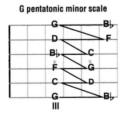

G pentatonic minor scale

There is nothing wrong with that. It does work, and there are plenty of note combinations to explore in that area. Just keep in mind that the *G* pentatonic minor scale also exists in every other position. **Ex. 9** (next page) shows the same scale in the fifth and the seventh positions. Explore the *G* blues sounds there.

EX. 9

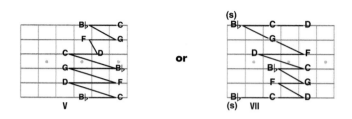

or

Remember that in position playing you sometimes stretch back or forward one fret (indicated now by a small "s" in the diagrams), extending the total span of a position to six frets.

The crucial realization is that this scale exists all over the fretboard. The chart in **Ex. 10** illustrates the idea, and it should be helpful to you as you experiment with the endless combinations of sounds that are possible with full access to these fundamental derivative tones of the *G* pentatonic minor scale. Most important, it should help you to realize more fully the "one key in all positions" concept, so that you don't always automatically go to that one most comfortable fretboard area. Ultimately, all areas of the fretboard should feel equally comfortable to you.

EX. 10

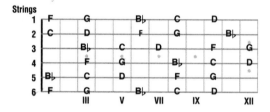

THE DORIAN MODE

In our first discussion we worked with the *C* Ionian mode (major scale), from which we extracted the major seventh arpeggio. Now, if we start the scale on the second degree (*D*) and ascend diatonically (scale-wise) to the next *D*, we get an entirely different scale, called the Dorian mode (**Ex. 11**).

Compared to the *D* major scale, this *D* Dorian scale (mode) has a flatted third (*F*, instead of *F♯*). The Dorian mode also has a natural sixth degree (in this case, *B*), the same as the major mode. The seventh degree is flatted (*C*, instead of *C♯* in this case). So we can define the Dorian mode as a minor scale (flatted third) with a natural sixth and a flatted seventh.

EX. 11

The Dorian mode is very common in nearly all styles of music. Perhaps you remember "Scarborough Fair," as recorded by Simon & Garfunkel. If you think of that melody, you'll get right into the Dorian frame of mind. Now play through the *D* Dorian fretboard pattern in the second position (**Ex. 12**).

You may have noticed that the notes are the same as those from the *C* Ionian mode. But you must think and hear *D* as the root. So, if you look back at the first part of this article, you will see that you can play all 12 Dorian modes in the second position by beginning (and naming) each mode from the second degree of each Ionian mode. In other words, the notes of the *G* Ionian mode can be selected to create an *A* Dorian mode, and so on.

EX. 12

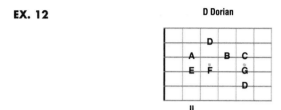

EX. 13

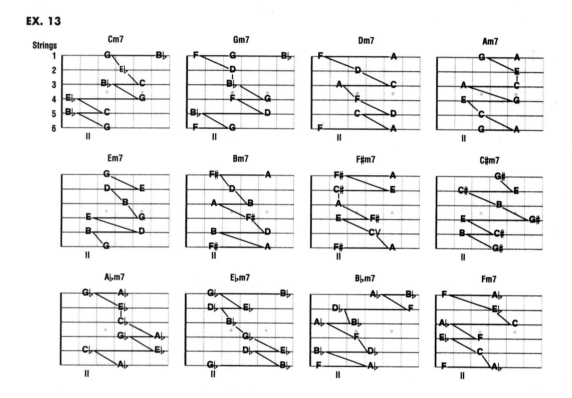

THE MINOR SEVENTH CHORD

Just as we isolated the first, third, fifth, and seventh degrees from the Ionian modes to derive the major seventh arpeggios, we will now isolate the first, third, fifth, and seventh degrees from the Dorian modes to derive another set of arpeggios. That combination of notes is the formula for the minor seventh chord. Amazingly, we can play all 12 minor seventh arpeggios in the second position, as in **Ex. 13** (above).

You also should be familiar with fingerings for the two chord types (major seventh and minor seventh) that we've discussed in order to cover the sounds of the scales we've been working with. In **Ex. 14**, two configurations for each chord type

EX. 14

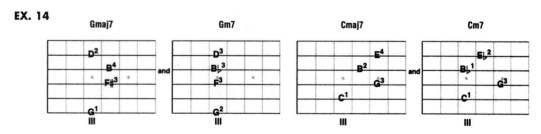

are shown: The first pair has the root note on the sixth string, and the second pair has the root on the fifth string.

These chord forms are movable, so once you learn them in the positions shown in **Ex. 14** (previous page) you can move them up or down the fretboard, determining the root either by the sixth-string note or by the fifth-string note, depending on which form you're using.

By now it should be clear to you that there is a special relationship between chords and scales. Chords are in fact derived from scales, and the mood of the chord reflects the mood of the scale from which it is derived. Every type of chord is related to a parent scale.

You can develop your chord/scale awareness by using your knowledge of the 12 Ionian modes, the 12 Dorian modes, and the chords that are based on those modes. Set aside some practice time to work with these modes and related scales. ■

FRETBOARD CHART

STRINGS

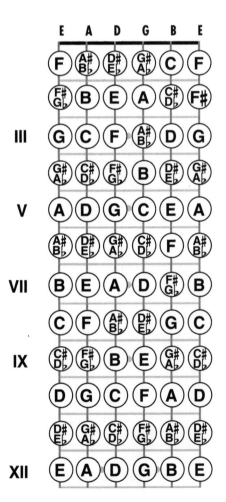

Chords 101

How to Major (and Minor) in the ABC's

BY RICK GARTNER

Chords are fundamental elements in the musical vocabulary of guitar players. The theoretical complexities and the manual contortions involved in the playing of some chords can bring a cold sweat to the brows of even experienced musicians. But just as with any branch of musical knowledge, there is an unintimidating place to begin, and there is always something more to learn.

Chord diagrams should convey information about which strings should be held down and where, which should be played open, and which should not be played at all. Unfortunately, a *Three Chords That Ruled the World* type of songbook may not include all of the necessary information, and a *Four Billion Guitar Chords* style book may overwhelm you with excess information. But if you first concentrate on learning a few properly fingered chord positions, you can avoid frustration and maximize the payoff of your practice time.

In the chord diagrams in **Ex. 1** (next page), the vertical lines represent the strings, with the lowest-sounding strings on the left, and the horizontal lines represent the frets. The thick horizontal line on the top is the nut, the notched fitting that guides the strings from the fretboard to the tuning pegs. The line below it represents the first fret.

Eric Clapton photo courtesy of PolyGram Records, 1985

TRACK 3

The dots tell you which strings to hold down, and at what fret. The number to the right of each dot specifies the left-hand finger that should stop the string, index through pinky being numbered 1 through 4, respectively. An "O" at the top of the diagram indicates a string that is to be played open, while an "X" indicates a string that should not be played.

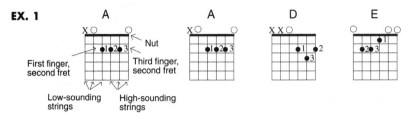

Chord diagrams follow this standard form wherever they appear. If the orientation is confusing at first, hold your guitar vertically so the fretboard faces you in order to duplicate the perspective. Sometimes you may encounter a horizontally oriented fretboard diagram, which is usually used for illustrating scales. Just keep your eye on the nut, and you'll be fine.

It's important to start off with the proper left-hand position since it has a significant effect on tone and finger movement. There are several rules of left-hand positioning that are essential to the development of good technique, and getting started correctly will save you from having to waste time correcting faulty technique later on. A few basic left-hand concepts:

1. Fingers should be arched at the joints so that the fingertips come down squarely on the strings (**Ex. 2a**). This is the opposite of "flat-fingered" playing, which decreases mobility and tends to bend or pull the strings, causing the notes to sound out of tune. However, it is necessary to flatten the first finger when playing *barre* chords, in which you stop two or more strings simultaneously.

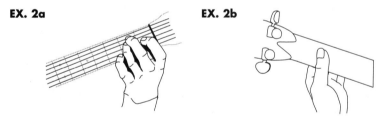

2. Fingers should contact the strings just slightly behind the frets; the farther away from the fret you press your finger, the more pressure is required to stop the string, and the likelihood of fret-buzzing is increased. (In some situations, such as the *A* chord in Ex. 1, it is impossible to stop all the notes immediately adjacent to the frets because of the complexity and the spatial requirements of certain fingering combinations.)

3. The thumb should stay near the middle of the back side of the neck, approximately opposite the first and second fingers (**Ex. 2b**). The thumb provides leverage and a point from which your hand can pivot. With your thumb wrapped around the neck, you lose this advantage.

4. Fingers should hover close to the strings when not fretting a note. Pulling fingers farther away from the fretboard actually takes more energy than leaving them close to the strings, and also increases the distance you must move them to bring them back into action. Economy of motion is a goal to which all guitarists should strive.

5. Your left arm should hang in a natural, relaxed manner. Your elbow should not rest against your body, but should be just far enough away to allow your hand to attack the fretboard at approximately a 90-degree angle.

The most important thing to remember when you play chords is that each note must be pressed down as a unit, not separately. (There are exceptions to this rule, which you'll encounter later. At first, though, it's critical to make all notes in your chords sound simultaneously.) Here's an exercise that I call the "slam-down drill" that is very helpful in establishing the habit of pressing down each chord as a unit.

First, press down an *A* chord. Second, lift your fingers off the strings about a half-inch as a unit, keeping the chord formation. Third, press your fingers back down onto the strings, firmly and quickly, keeping the formation. If any of your fingers miss the proper position in the chord, correct them and repeat the drill.

When you feel comfortable with the *A* chord, do the same exercise with the *D* and *E* chords. Then practice the slam-down drill while changing chords. Start with *A*, lift, and press down the *D* chord. Release, then press down the *E* chord. Keep it slow, and correct any mistakes as you go.

The next step is to strum as you do the drill. Keep your strum even and in steady rhythm; don't stop your strum if you miss a chord. Force your left hand to catch up with your right.

After a bit of practice, you'll probably start to feel comfortable with these basic chord positions. If not, you may want to consider alternate fingerings. There may be several possible fingerings for a chord, and which you choose should depend on the comfort of your hand and which fingering works best with the chords that precede and follow.

The size of your hand and the width of your instrument's neck have a significant effect on whether a particular fingering feels comfortable. A classical (nylon-string) guitar has a considerably wider neck (about 20%) than a steel-string guitar. Consequently, playing chords on a classical guitar often requires that you make longer reaches, but the wider fretboard allows you more room to maneuver on closely bunched fingering combinations. How that affects your playing depends on the size and shape of your hand. For example, a person with large hands usually finds the open *A* chord difficult to play, especially within the confines of a steel-string fretboard.

Ex. 3 shows three different fingerings for the basic *A* chord. The first is the most commonly used, and the other two have fingering adjustments some might find more comfortable. In the middle diagram, the curved line surrounding the two adjacent dots indicates that both strings are to be pressed down with the same finger (the first finger in this case). Of course, you'll have to flatten your first finger to hold both strings down.

The most comfortable fingering is not necessarily the one to choose. From a musical and technical point of view, two of the most important things to consider are: Which fingering best facilitates changing to other chords, and which fingering allows you to throw in embellishments or melodic material with your left hand? The *G* chord provides a good example for these musical considerations.

In **Ex. 4** (next page) there are three fingerings for the basic *G* chord. I strongly recommend the first, although many players use the second with good results. The third is sometimes taught to beginners simply because it is easier, but this fingering is very awkward from a musical and technical standpoint. I only include it as an example of a bad habit that many players learn for the sake of expediency.

I recommend the first fingering because it best facilitates two common chord changes, *G* to *C*, and *G* to *G7*. Much less finger movement is required to make those chord changes when you use the first fingering. The *G* to *G7* chord change is the best example—moving from the first *G* fingering to *G7* requires the changing of just one note, while you must shift the position of your entire hand to make the change using the second *G* fingering.

A very lovely embellishment, *G* suspended (*Gsus4*), is also more readily available from the first *G* fingering. On the bottom line of **Ex. 4** are diagrams for *C*, *G7*, and *Gsus4* chords. Try changing to these chords from each of the first two *G* fingerings and compare the difference in the movement needed. Most people who shy away from the first *G* fingering do so because their fourth finger (the pinky) just won't behave. That's really not a good enough reason, because with practice you can learn to control your little finger.

EX. 4

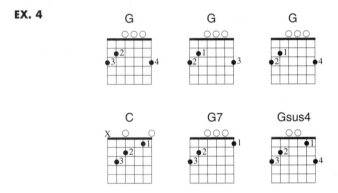

Let's take a look at one more chord, *D*. There are two fingerings for the *D* chord in **Ex. 5**, as well as diagrams for the *Dsus4* embellishment. Both of the *D* fingerings work well, and each has a special advantage. The first allows you to easily lift your finger off the first string, which gives you another embellishment to the *D* chord. The second fingering allows you to reach out to the 5th fret on the top string (with your pinky), which is a nice addition to the sound of the basic *D* chord. To play the *Dsus4*, add your fourth finger to the first *D* fingering or add your third to the second *D* fingering.

EX. 5

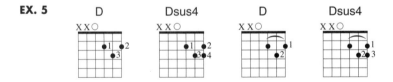

Of course, any decision about fingering is entirely your own. But keep in mind that any song will require at least a couple of chord changes. Although one fingering for a chord may seem easier by itself, it may prove to be very awkward when you try to change chords in the middle of a song. Your decisions about fingering should be based partially on what feels comfortable, and partially on what makes the most musical sense.

Now you're on your way to building a solid foundation for playing chords. I've introduced only a few chords so far, and while they actually can serve as all you need to accompany a large number of songs, there will come a time when you want to play more chords. One way to increase your chord vocabulary with a minimum of effort is to learn a couple of movable formations, which you can move from position to position.

Before we start moving things around on your fretboard, let's take a look at how notes are named on the guitar. **Ex 5.1** shows the note names for the first 12 frets on the *A* string. Note that some fret locations have two names, and others have only one. Also note that while the single-named locations seem to alternate with the double ones, the pattern appears irregular. The reason for this will become apparent to you if you look at the keyboard of a piano or synthesizer. Much of the language of music was contrived to describe what happens on a keyboard, not on a fretboard, and this is just one notable example.

EX. 5.1

A—A#(B♭)—B—C—C#(D♭)—D—D#(E♭)—E—F—F3(G♭)—G—G#(A♭)—A

The frets on your guitar are spaced at half-step intervals. You can identify any note on a given string if you know the name of the open string, locate it on the chromatic scale in Ex. 5.1, and then count upwards the same number of frets as the note in question is from the nut. Suppose that you want to identify the note located at the 3rd fret on the sixth string, which is the low *E* string. Locate *E* in Ex. 6, and count up three half-steps, remembering that *F#/G♭* count as only one half-step. Presto! The note you're looking for is *G*. A similar approach will work to determine the name of a movable chord as you move it up or down the neck.

For a chord to be movable, its fingering must allow it to preserve the same relationship of the notes as you move it. A chord that uses open strings requires moving the open strings the same distance as the fretted notes. (The open strings would sound the same notes if you only moved the rest of the chord.) The quality of a chord doesn't change as you move it, only the letter name. A *C* minor chord will still be a minor chord no matter where you place it; it just won't be a *C* minor chord anymore.

Some of the easiest movable chords to finger are those that are played on the first three or four strings. **Ex. 6** shows both a major and a minor chord formation. Just as we identified a single note by using the chromatic scale, we can identify the letter name of a movable chord anywhere on the neck. For example, if you move the *F* chord up one fret, it becomes an *F#* (or *G♭*) chord. Move it up another fret, and it becomes a *G* chord. Similarly, if you move the *Bm* chord up one fret, it becomes a *Cm* chord. It's still a minor chord; just the letter name changes. If you move it up another fret, the result is a *C#m* chord.

EX. 6

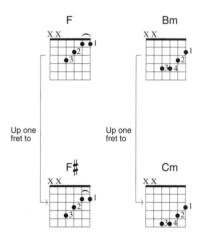

Perhaps there's a song that you always dismissed as being too hard because it had an *F#* chord in it. You can solve many such problems by becoming familiar with the chromatic scale and just one or two movable chord formations. ∎

Family Ties
WHERE DO CHORDS COME FROM?

BY JESSE GRESS

Which came first: the chord or the scale? Any chord can certainly be viewed as a stand-alone entity, but there's more to the big picture. Chords come from scales, or more specifically, harmonized scales. And they have big families. Let's zero in on two scales — *C* major and *C* minor — and check out what their harmonic relatives are up to.

Joe Pass photo courtesy of Pablo Records

MEET THE PARENTS

Scale harmony begins with scales, and every scale has its own formula, measured in half-steps and whole-steps. (A half-step is a distance of one fret; a whole-step spans two frets.) Each scale note gets a designated number, called a scale step or degree. Each numbered scale degree corresponds with its intervallic distance above the root. In other words, step two is a second above the root (*C* to *D,* in the key of *C* major), step three is a third above the root (*C* to *E*), step four is a fourth (*C* to *F*), and so on.

    Examples 1a and **Ex. 1b** (next page) show the *C* major and *C* minor scales, their half- and whole-step formulas, and their Roman-numeral scale degrees: I, II, III, IV, V, VI, and VII (major) and I, II, ♭III, IV, V, ♭VI, and ♭VII (minor). Both formulas — laid out here on the fifth string to accommodate our upcoming harmonies — are applicable to all 12 keys. Get to know them.

EX. 1a

EX. 1b

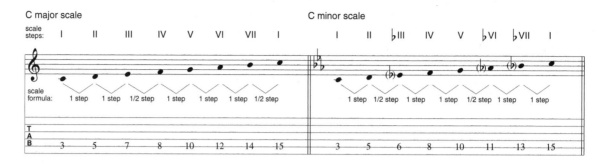

MEET THE KIDS

Traditionally, chords are built using diatonic harmony, which means that the scale is harmonized with itself. The process begins with the construction of harmonic intervals of a third on each scale step. Essentially, the *C* major and *C* minor scales in **Examples 2a** and **2b** are stacked on top of themselves starting on their respective third scale steps and continuing through the octave (the scale's eighth note, which has the same note name as the root). You can think of this as simultaneously tracking each scale from two different points on two adjacent strings.

Two types of third intervals emerge from each scale. (The original notes of both scales are redesignated as the roots from which all the harmonies are calculated.) The *C* major scale produces major thirds (root–3, or two whole-steps) on scale steps I, IV, and V, and minor thirds (root–♭3, or one-and-one-half steps) on scale steps II, III, VI, and VII. In *C* minor, these change to minor thirds on scale steps I, II, IV, and V, and to major thirds on steps ♭III, ♭VI, and ♭VII. Again, this applies to all major and minor keys.

EX. 2a

EX. 2b

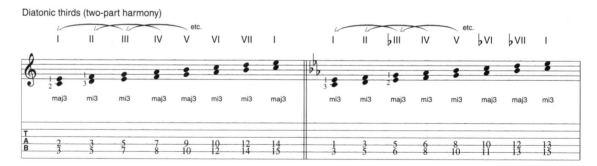

MEET THE RELATIVES

While two stacked thirds can suggest a chord sound, the first legitimate chordal unit is the three-note triad. Triads are built by stacking each scale on top of its third harmonies beginning on the fifth scale step — a diatonic third above the third degree — and continuing up to the octave. You can think of this as simultaneously tracking each scale from three different points on three adjacent strings. **Examples 3a** and **3b** show root-position voicings for the diatonic triads related to the *C* major and *C* minor scales.

Three types of triads are derived from each harmonized scale. In major keys, scale steps I, IV, and V are major triads (root–3–5), steps II, III, and VI are minor triads (root–♭3–5), and step VII is known as a diminished triad (root–♭3–♭5). In minor keys, steps I, IV, and V are minor, steps ♭III, ♭VI, and ♭VII are major, and step II is diminished. The diatonic formula automatically adjusts the triads to the same specs, regardless of key. You can use the Roman-numeral step indicators to convey all necessary information for diatonic chord progressions, such as I–IV–V and I–VIm–IIm–V.

EX. 3a   **EX. 3b**

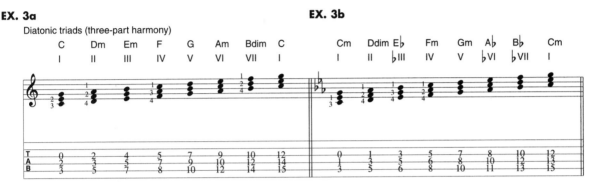

SEVENTH HEAVEN

Continuing the process, we add another row of diatonic thirds on top of our triads starting on the seventh scale step — a diatonic third above the fifth degree — for the four-note seventh-chord harmonies in **Examples 4a** and **4b**. By now, you may have noticed that the starting point for each new layer of harmonized thirds is every other note of the original scale. Look closely and you'll see every triad from **Examples 3a** and **3b** — starting with *Em* (III of *C* major) and *E♭m* (♭III of *C* minor) — nested snugly on top of each original scale tone. These triad-over-bass-note "slash chords" (shown in parentheses) are valuable for breaking down hard-to-play root-position seventh chords into smaller components. You can also think of this as playing each scale starting from four different points on four adjacent strings.

Each harmonized scale yields four types of seventh chords. In *C* major, scale steps I and IV are major-seventh chords (root–3–5–7), steps II, III, and VI are minor seventh chords (root–♭3–5–♭7), step V is a dominant seventh chord (root–3–5–♭7), and step VII is a minor seventh–flat five chord (root–♭3–♭5–♭7). In *C* minor, steps I, IV, and V are minor seventh chords, ♭III and ♭VI are major sevenths, ♭VII is a dominant seventh, and II is a minor seventh–flat five. Once again, this applies to all major and minor keys.

EX. 4a   **EX. 4b**

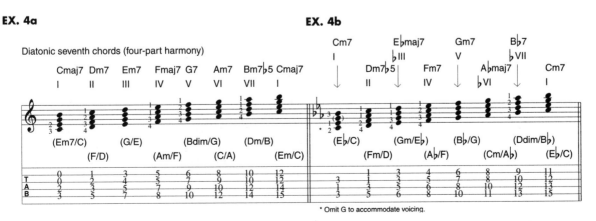

* Omit G to accommodate voicing.

GO NINERS

Adding a fourth line of harmonized thirds gives us the five-note diatonic ninth chords in **Examples 5a** and **5b**.

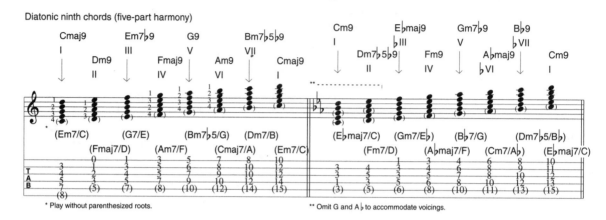

EX. 5a

EX. 5b

* Play without parenthesized roots.

** Omit G and Ab to accommodate voicings.

It's nearly impossible to grasp these root-position voicings in their entirety, but if we omit the root of each chord, we're left with the seventh-chord voicings from Examples 4a and 4b, starting with the IIIm7 and bIIImaj7 chords. Using this formula, we can deduce the formulas below—read *Em7/C* as "*Em7* over *C*": an *Em7* chord played over a *C* note:

Key of C major

Cmaj9 = Em7/C
Dm9 = Fmaj7/D
Em7b9 = G7/E
Fmaj9 = Am7/F
G9 = Bm7b5/G
Am9 = Cmaj7/A
Bm7b5b9 = Dm7/B

Key of C minor

Cm9 = Ebmaj7/C
Dm7b5b9 = Fm7/D
Ebmaj9 = Gm7/E
Fm9 = Abmaj7/F
Gm7b9 = Bb7/G
Abmaj9 = Cm7/A
Bb9 = Dm7b5/B.

Like all of our diatonic harmonies so far, this applies to all major and minor keys.

Additionally, the top three notes of each seventh chord form another row of diatonic triads, this time a fifth above each root. From this perspective, *Cmaj9 = G/C, Dm9 = Am/D,* and so on. Note that all of these triad-over-bass slash chords are third-less.

AT EASE

So far, we've only looked at root-position chord voicings. Some of these — especially seventh and ninth chords — can be painfully "stretchy" or voiced too closely together for some situations. Let's make them easier to play. The remaining examples respell each harmonized scale using voicings and fingerings that fit like a pair of old gloves. All are built from our parent *C* major and *C* minor scales.

Examples 6a and 6b feature first-inversion triad harmonies (3–5–root) played on the second, third, and fourth strings. Follow the second string and name that chord.

EX. 6a   **EX. 6b**

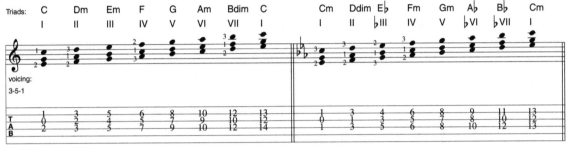

Examples 7a and 7b show second-inversion triads guitarists from Jimi Hendrix to Mark Knopfler have embraced. The game of root tag jumps to the third string. Use the optional parenthetical roots to create four-note voicings (root–5–root–3), or leave off the second string for heavy root–5–root power chords.

EX. 7a   **EX. 7b**

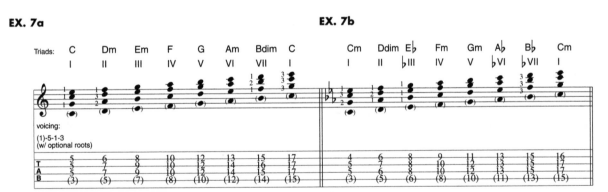

The seventh-chord harmonies in **Examples 8a, 8b, 9a,** and **9b** (next page) are spread out into comfy root–5–7–3 and root–7–3–5 voicings, standard fare in R&B and jazz.

By omitting the 5 from each chord in **Examples 10a** and **10b**, we arrive at a manageable set of fingerings for our ninth-chord scale harmony. The dominant-ninth V chord is funk-, blues-, and cool-jazz-approved, while the major-ninth (I and IV) and minor-ninth (II and VI) voicings sound lush and lovely.

Now that you know where chords come from (tell a friend!), you can use them in hundreds of new configurations, both individually and collectively.

EX. 8a

EX. 8b

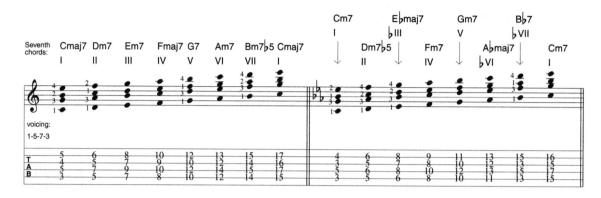

EX. 9a

EX. 9b

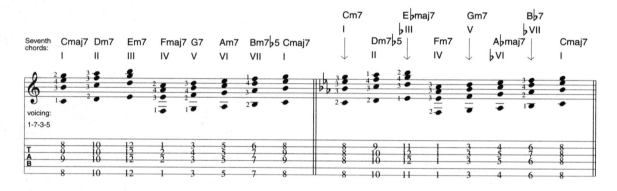

EX. 10a

EX. 10b

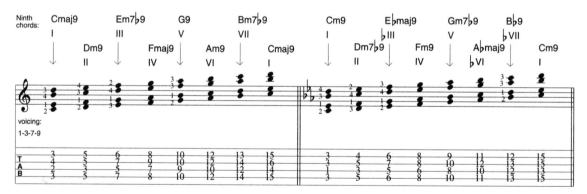

FINAL TIPS:

- Transpose all harmonized scales to all keys.
- Transfer harmonized scales to adjacent string groups.
- Practice playing harmonized scales in the same position.
- Arpeggiate harmonized scales—play the chord notes individually, in sequence— to produce melodic sequences.
- Use harmonized scales to create modal vamps and chord solos.
- Incorporate new voicings into familiar chord progressions.
- Write your own chord book.

Strummin' with Style

HOW TO PLAY SONGS AND MAKE MUSIC

BY RICK GARTNER

Basic chord strumming is an excellent way to get started toward playing a few songs. After mastering the essential skill of keeping a rhythmic strum going while making a few chord changes, most strummers start thinking about becoming pickers, but it's usually difficult for them to find the right technique to practice next.

A logical step is to incorporate individual bass notes into simple strumming patterns. The introduction of bass notes into your strumming patterns not only adds variety to the sound of your playing, but it also greatly increases your potential repertoire of songs. Of course, it requires considerably more control to pick out individual bass notes between strumming strokes, but just give your hands a chance and they will amaze you with their hidden talents.

One type of strum that is used extensively in bluegrass, folk, and country songs is a "bass-brush" or "boom-chick" technique, which is played by picking a bass note and then brushing down across the strings. "Boom-chick" strumming is most commonly played with a flatpick, but it can also be done very effectively with your thumb and fingers, with the possible addition of a thumbpick. The illustrations in **Ex. 1** (next page) show both the flatpick and the thumb-and-fingers approaches.

Cesar Rosas of Los Lobos photo courtesy of Shure Inc.

TRACK 4

Whichever approach you take, you should think of the bass note and the chord brush as being played with separate motions. If you're playing with a flat-pick, play the bass note with a quick, precise wrist flick downwards, and follow that with a crisp downstroke across the first four strings. If you're using the thumb-and-fingers approach, play the bass note with your thumb (or thumbpick) and then brush down across the first four strings with whichever fingers feel most comfortable. For optimum control, the thumb should move from the joint labeled "active joint" in **Ex. 1** as you strike the bass note. Don't play the chord brush with your thumb because it must hover near the bass strings, prepared to play the next bass note.

EX. 1

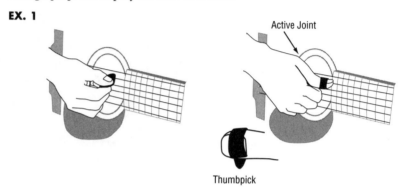

Active Joint

Thumbpick

Ex. 2 shows a basic "boom-chick" strum. Try to count as you play, and remember that the bass note and the chord brush are played with separate motions. To get the feel of the strum and to develop initial control of the bass strokes, begin by limiting yourself to playing just one bass note on the fifth string as shown in the tablature. Play all bass notes with downstrokes.

EX. 2

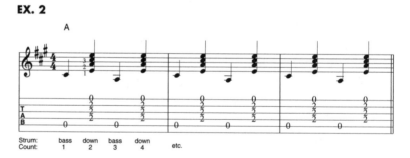

The most common pattern of bass notes in both "boom-chick" strumming and in fingerpicking is referred to as "alternating bass." For example, if you play a bass note on the fifth string and then play a chord brush, you can play the next bass note on the fourth string, followed by another chord brush. Your next bass note would then be played on the fifth string again, thus establishing a bass pattern that alternates between the fifth string and the fourth string. Again, to

EX. 3

develop control, limit yourself to a two-note alternating bass pattern (fifth to fourth string), as shown in **Ex. 3**.

Try the next set of chord changes **(Ex. 4)** and notice that on the *G* and the *E* chords, the bass alternates between the sixth and the fourth strings. The sixth-to-fourth bass pattern requires still more control, but it's well worth the effort.

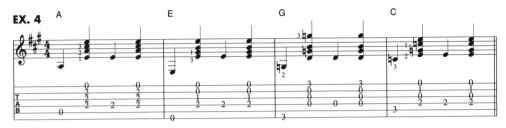

Among the many songs that go well with an alternating bass strum is "Wabash Cannonball" **(Ex. 5)**. If the alternating bass is giving you trouble, you can still play the song by using the "boom-chick" strum and keeping your bass on the fifth string throughout the song. If it's the sixth-to-fourth alternating bass pattern (*G* chord) that's debilitating your digits, you can play a fifth-to-fourth bass pattern through-

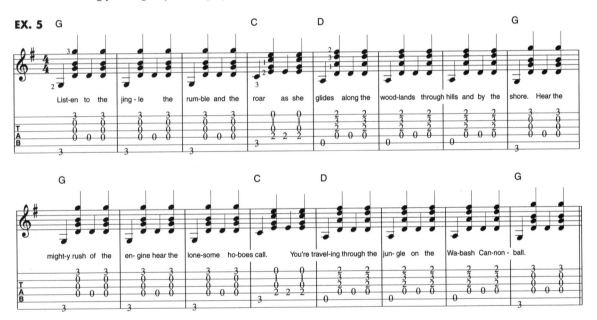

out. Don't be dismayed if everything falls apart when you first try to sing as you play the new strum—it takes a while to make all the necessary cranial connections.

Once you're comfortable with these basic strumming techniques, you can start adding some advanced techniques. Ornaments and embellishments are stylistic touches that can add an individualistic quality to your playing. In a very general sense, ornaments and embellishments are notes that fill out and color your basic chords as you play them. While it takes a good deal of theoretical background and playing experience to employ the more sophisticated chord substitutions and extensions, there are some convenient departures from the mundane that require only minor fingering adjustments.

One versatile style-expanding technique is called *hammering on*, a term that is descriptive of the motions involved in the technique. You can play hammer-on notes either as part of a chord or in a run of single notes from any position on the fretboard.

First, let's get the feel of doing a hammer-on from a single note. Place the first finger of your right hand on the sixth string, just behind the 2nd fret. Using your picking hand, play that note with the thumb or a pick to produce a strong, loud note. Play the note again, and immediately bring the second finger of your right hand down just behind the third fret—"hammer" it down hard and fast to produce the second note (**Ex. 6**). You get two notes for the price of one, because you only

EX. 6

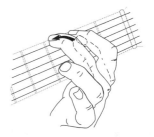

pick the note that precedes the hammer-on note. You must bring your hammering finger down hard and fast—and hold it down firmly to get a good hammer-on note.

An excellent way to incorporate hammer-on notes into your playing is through alternating bass strumming. Form a *C* chord with your left hand (**Ex. 7**). Lift your

EX. 7

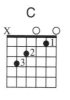
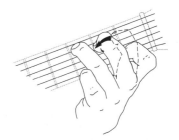

second finger off the fourth string so it hovers directly over its normal position in the *C* chord. Play the fourth string open, then hammer your second finger down onto its position in the chord, keeping your other fingers firmly in place.

Next, do that same hammer-on note from the *C* chord, and follow it with a downward strum. After the strum, play the fifth-string bass note, and follow with another strum. Repeat the entire sequence slowly, keeping a steady beat. The two notes involved with the hammer-on must occur evenly, and within one beat. The only thing is that you must lift your second finger just before each hammer-on note. A common hammer-on lick for the *G* chord is shown in **Ex. 8**; hammer the fifth string on the *G* chord. Both hammer-on licks are shown in **Ex. 9**.

EX. 8

Next, try out the hammer-on licks in "Wabash Cannonball" (**Ex. 10**). Once you get control of hammer-ons, you can plug them in whenever they seem to fit. Play them as part of an original song or arrangement, or use them as improvisational elements. ■

EX. 9

Strum: bass down bass down etc.
Count: 1 2 3 & 4

EX. 10

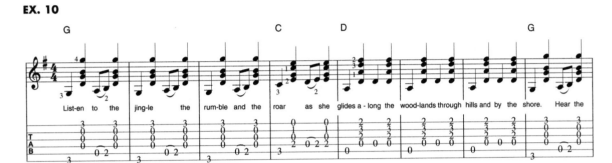

List-en to the jing-le the rum-ble and the roar as she glides a - long the wood-lands through hills and by the shore. Hear the

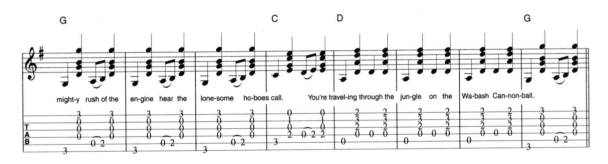

might-y rush of the en-gine hear the lone-some ho-boes call. You're travel-ing through the jun-gle on the Wa-bash Can-non-ball.

Sweet & Low

USING BASS RUNS

BY RICK GARTNER

Expanding your bag of guitaristic tricks is always exciting. One way to go beyond the basic chord-strumming accompaniment is to learn some bass runs to vary the texture of your sound and provide a feeling of connection between chords. Many very familiar-sounding bass runs are actually nothing more than scale segments that can be employed in any key.

Sioux Sandberg photo courtesy of Michael Manson/Suit Guy Records

In the key of *C*, the last four notes of the major scale are *G*, *A*, *B*, and *C*. (For fingerings of all 12 major scales, see page 21, **Ex. 4**.) An exercise for learning that typical bass-run pathway into the *C* chord is shown in **Ex. 1** (next page). Each note and strum receives one count in 4/4 time. Play the exercise slowly and repeat it until you can keep the beat steady. Pay close attention to the fingerings, shown in the small numbers next to the notes. In this example, the fingering numbers correspond to the fret numbers.

Notice that the last note of the run—*C*—conveniently fits into the *C* chord. Finger the entire *C* chord when you play the *C* bass note, since you follow that final bass note with a downward strum of the *C* chord.

TRACK 5

EX. 1

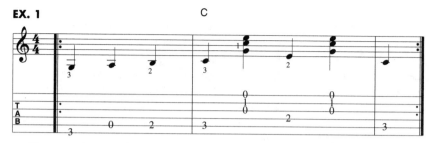

The same bass pathway may be used—moving down from the C note this time—to lead into the G chord, as in **Ex. 2**. The last note in this exercise—D—may be used to extend the length of the bass run to five notes. Those five notes, which lead into the G chord, are the *first* five of the G major scale, played in descending order.

EX. 2

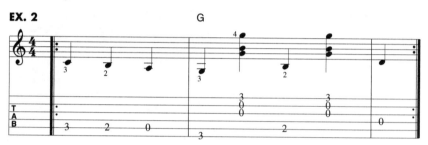

The exercise in **Ex. 3** is identical in concept to Ex. 1, but this time the last four notes of the F major scale are used to lead into the F chord. Notice that the fretting and fingering of the run in Ex. 3 is the same as that of Ex. 1, except that the run in Ex. 3 is played one string higher.

EX. 3

The same pathway that leads up to the F chord leads down to the C chord, as shown in **Ex. 4**. Just as in Ex. 2, the addition of a final note—G this time—extends the run to five notes: the first five of the C major scale, played in descending order.

EX. 4

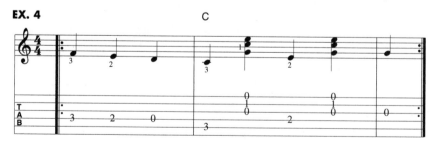

Since the C, F, and G major scales are composed predominately of the same notes (common tones), you can combine segments of those scales to create bass runs that connect the C, F, and G chords.

The "boom-chick" strum in the second measure of the previous examples is a good accompaniment pattern for many songs, especially when you develop firm control of the bass notes. The chord will determine the note choice, but fifth-string and fourth-string bass notes will sound good in virtually all basic guitar chords. Conversely, the sixth string, *E*, which is left open in many basic chords, sounds awful when played as a bass note against a *D* or *F* chord, and is at best distracting against an open *C* chord. But when the sixth string is fretted in a chord such as *G*, the sixth-string bass note is effective.

You can add a lot of personality and style to your playing by making full use of the bass notes available in and near chords, and these fit nicely with bass runs such as those in the first four examples. It's now time to combine the two in a song.

Many familiar-sounding bass runs are major-scale segments that are three to five notes long, and they require only minor adjustments in fingering. In fact, many runs start with a bass note in the chord you're going from, and end with a bass note in the chord you're going to. You only have to move your fingers out of the chord formation for one or two notes.

Don't feel compelled to connect every chord change with a bass run—that kind of busy accompaniment can confuse you and your listeners. To play the song below, "Banks of the Ohio," use a boom-chick strum. The chords and lyrics of the song are shown in **Ex. 5**.

After you feel comfortable with these chord changes, play the five-measure excerpt in **Ex. 6**, which includes chord-connecting bass runs. Then plug those five measures into the accompaniment pattern in Ex. 5, starting where you see the asterisk (measures 9-13). When you can play it smoothly, you might want to experiment by using the same run elsewhere, or by inventing runs of your own.

EX. 6

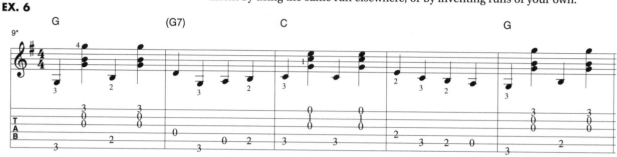

Notice that this version of the melody—there are several—is composed of only five notes: the first five of the *G* major scale (the song is in the key of *G* major). For reference, those five notes are written in **Ex. 7**.

EX. 7

The bass runs in Ex. 6 contain only the first *four* notes of the *G* major scale. You can see why major scales, and scales in general, have long been considered fundamental for instrumentalists and singers. ∎

The Flatpicker's Rhythm Method

SIMPLE IS BEST—MOST OF THE TIME

BY DAN CRARY

There is a misconception among musicians that accompaniment is just something you do while you're waiting for a chance to play a lead, or when you can't do anything else. Not so! Playing solid, appropriate accompaniment is a challenge worthy of careful study. The payoff is music that is beautiful and satisfying.

BASIC RHYTHM

Take a look at the basic rhythm lick in 4/4 time (**Ex. 1**, next page) for *C*, *F*, and *G* major. I have a little fun with workshop participants by introducing this lick with the promise that I'm about to show them one of the most powerful, least-used, exotic, and "inside" accompaniment licks known to guitarists.

Doc Watson photo by A. Maxwell

The irony is this: That lick *is* rarely used, not because no one knows it, but because everyone thinks it's too simple or basic. Quite often, I tell experienced players that their accompaniment needs more of this basic lick in it. In traditional flatpicking music, this bass/strum/bass/strum move is fundamental. Learning it now is not a *step* to something important, it *is* important, and is worth learning right.

TRACK 6

EX. 1

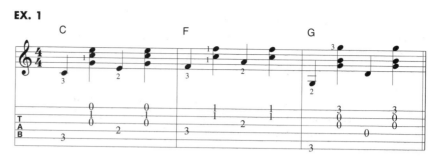

A solid, crisp delivery of this rhythm lick will improve your solo playing because its discipline will carry over to solos. Your accompaniment will help give the lead player the confidence to do his or her best. Your singing will sound far better with a solid rhythm lick behind it. This is one of those "things they never tell you" at the right time, so you're hearing it from me now. Here's how to play this lick with a flat-pick *right* and forever.

First, notice that the first bass note is the "name" note (the root) of the chord. This should be a rule: Play the name note first. The alternate bass note can be any note from the chord (the root, 3rd, or 5th). Later on, I'll explain why certain alternating bass notes sound different from others, but for now just make sure it's one of the notes that define the chord.

Second—and this is something nobody ever told me—when you strum the chord on beats *two* and *four* of the measure, strum only the top three strings. This is not a hard and fast rule, but it helps. Try it both ways. If you play the entire chord, it's not as clean a sound as a strum of just the top three strings. In any case, your left hand should hold the whole chord so the bass note can sustain.

Third—and this is very "inside"—try squeezing the pick just a little tighter (by pushing against the pick with your thumb) on the bass note, then easing off and playing a little looser on the strum. The strum should still be definite and precise, but a little gentler and smoother than the bass note.

Here's one additional tip that may help when you're first struggling with chord changes. It's always a problem to change chords when the beat presses on without waiting for you. But in the basic pattern, the first beat of the measure calls not for a whole chord, but only for one note, the bass note. So when you make a chord change, grab the bass note first, play it on time, and finger the rest of the chord with your left hand *during* the first beat of the measure. That extra little bit of time is precisely what experienced players use to find the rest of the chord position with the left hand.

EX. 2

Of course, there is a lot more to be said about the basic rhythm lick. I'll show you some variations, but let's make a slight but useful digression: Consider the melody in **Ex. 2**. Do you recognize the tune? It's a snippet of "Home Sweet Home," a tune that serves to make an important point: The bass/strum accompaniment pattern can get you started playing tunes and breaks. **Ex. 3** shows the same tune with the melody notes used in place of the bass notes of the basic pattern.

Here's an assignment: Go back and play the basic pattern. Then play a tune you know. Then play the combination. Compare all three, and get a feel for how they fit together.

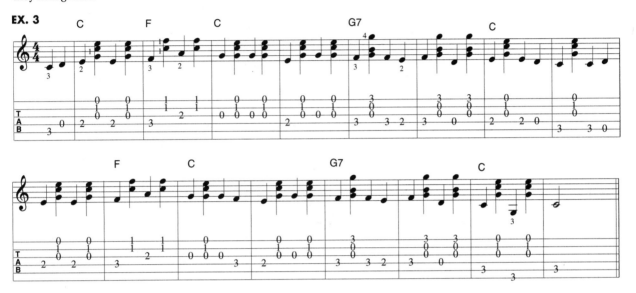

VARIATIONS ON THE BASIC RHYTHM

Now you're ready for some variations on the basic rhythm lick. First, try playing a "back stroke" on the *first string* after the strum (**Ex. 4**). Notice that the timing does not change. The added up-stroke with the pick has to be inserted into the basic *one, two, three, four* count of the measure, making it *one, two-and, three, four-and,* with the back strokes falling on the "ands." Here's another of those inside tricks Grandma never told you: On the up-stroke after the strum, play *only the first string* of the chord. Try it with more strings, and you'll see that the single-string stroke is much cleaner.

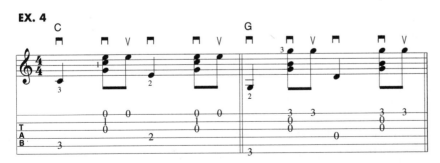

Now alter the basic pattern with a quick up-stroke after the bass note (see **Ex. 5** on next page). Notice that the basic pattern is still there, and the time value of each of those original elements remains, with the added variations sort of slipped in between the cracks.

EX. 5

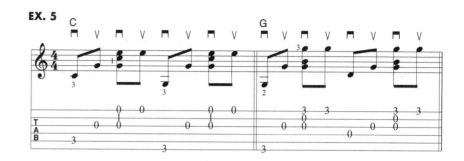

Next try changing the bass notes of the basic pattern by playing a hammer-on. Play the open string, then finger the fretted note hard enough to sound against the fret—without picking again. Or, try substituting a pull-off. Pick a higher note, then "snap" the left-hand finger off the string to make the lower note sound. Here again, the left hand does the work. Don't pick the lower note. These variations are demonstrated in **Ex. 6**.

EX. 6

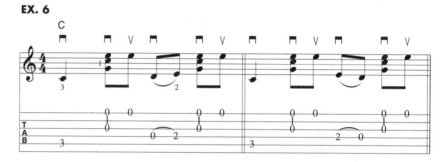

As you experiment, here's a caution: These variations can make good music, or they can make a mess. The trick is, remember the basic pattern. Play it as a basic position to which you return often as you play accompaniment. Use the variations sparingly, for short passages of a measure or two, then get back to the beat, that solid core sound of the basic pattern. The variations are powerful in providing variety and flexibility, but they are deadly in long passages. If overused, they tend to pull players away from a solid commitment to the beat.

I know it's hard to remember everything when you're starting out. So let me suggest this: Consider that your main task at first is to get your mental metronome working, to make those musical beats start pounding steadily in your brain. As your right hand gets more familiar with the basic pattern, discipline it to follow that regular beat in your head. After you've achieved a little steadiness, try adding some of the variations—sparingly—to your accompaniments.

Keep up the good work and don't get discouraged. You'll get there! Pat Flynn's fingers probably hurt when he first started, too.

PLAYING SLOW TEMPOS

Fireplaces on winter nights, quiet conversations while the snow falls outside, peaceful hiding out on February weekends, and moments of escape from the chaos out there—these times are rare and priceless. And they need some music to fit. Soft music, quiet music, *slow* music.

Perhaps our friendly critics are right when they say flatpicking needs some of the variety, and pretty stuff, that playing slower material might provide. Here are some ideas for playing slow accompaniment.

It seems like it ought to be easy; if it's hard to play fast, it must be easy to play slow. One of the ironies of the guitar is that *nothing* is easy to play well. It's just that slow playing requires a different discipline than fast playing does.

What kind of discipline? Precision, careful attention to tempo, and a very steady—yet smooth and expressive—execution. Ask a fiddle player about the challenge of playing waltzes; the same set of challenges applies to any slow music on the guitar.

First, notice that some of the rhythm licks we've discussed earlier lend themselves well to slow tempos. The back-stroke variation of the basic lick (**Ex. 7**) works nicely, especially if you stretch out the strum just a little, and play the timing very precisely. For 3/4 time **Ex. 8** works about the same.

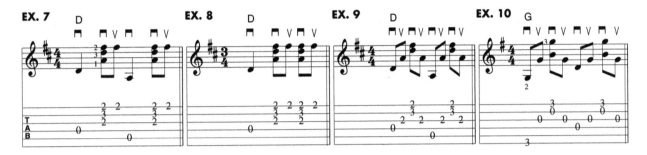

For a nice variation, consider the double back-stroke variation at slow tempos, where it actually works better: **Ex. 9** in *D; G* (**Ex. 10**); *C* (**Ex. 11**); and *E* (**Ex. 12**). Two rules: Play the name note on count "one" of the measure; and each of the back-strokes should be played on *one string.* As always, it's a good idea to break up any potential monotony by alternating with the basic bass-strum rhythm lick.

Some other standard accompaniment moves sound good played slow. Hammering on one bass note in a four-beat measure (**Ex. 13**) seems to work especially well, as it does in a three-beat measure (**Ex. 14**). Similarly, a very deliberate strum on the first beat in 4/4 is a good effect (**Ex. 15**).

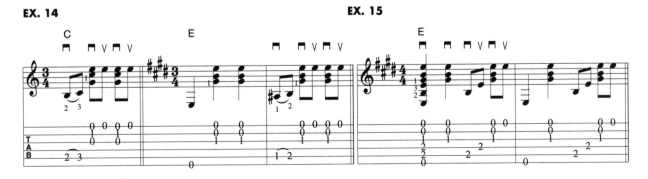

Slow chords can be pretty when played with partial fingerings adjacent to open strings. You'll see a few positions provided in **Ex. 16**, and two sample progressions in **Ex. 17**.

EX. 16

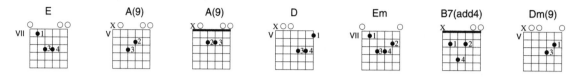

EX. 17

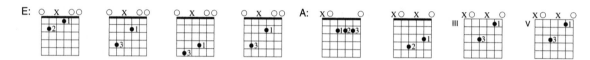

Overall, the hardest part of playing slow rhythm is keeping the tempo steady and maintaining a sustained flow or smoothness. For the timing, I recommend buying and using a metronome when you practice slow music. Practice? Yes, I'm afraid careful attention to the subtleties of slow music requires systematic practice, especially to set a steady and true tempo. I recently took my own advice about the metronome and found it to be a very humbling experience. (My timing also has improved.)

On the issue of sustain and smooth flow, you might try drawing out the arpeggios and strums a little longer than you normally would, while preserving an accurate tempo. This sounds a little contradictory, but it seems to work, and the effect is to stretch and smooth out the flow of the music.

A change of pace is not only welcome, but some slow stuff makes the fast and furious stuff sound even faster—and less furious. ∎

Digital Domain

FINGERPICKING BASICS FOR ACCOMPANIMENT AND MELODY

BY RICK GARTNER & HAPPY TRAUM

When the first hint of boredom lessens your motivation for learning music, working on a new song or technique can reawaken your interest. Hopefully, boredom will arise only after you've mastered (or nearly mastered) the material you've been working on. It's important to move up to the next level *before* you develop an aversion to the music you know. Otherwise, the repertoire you've worked so hard to learn becomes just "those same old songs." Once you can make a few chord changes with a consistent, steady strum, you're ready to try some fingerpicking.

Fingerpicking can be broadly defined as any style of playing in which the fingers pluck the strings. So about the only styles not covered by that definition are flat-picking and basic strumming. We'll narrow down this discussion into two fingerpicking categories: (1) accompaniment pattern picking, and (2) ragtime and blues picking (solos and accompaniment).

Son Thomas photo by Axel Küstner, 1980

ACCOMPANIMENT PATTERN PICKING

The best place to start is accompaniment pattern picking. The principles of hand positioning and attack (picking motion) for this technique are identical to those used in more complex styles, but there are other, potentially more frustrating technical challenges that can be temporarily avoided by focusing on pattern picking. That will give you a solid foundation of fingerpicking skills.

TRACK 7

EX. 1

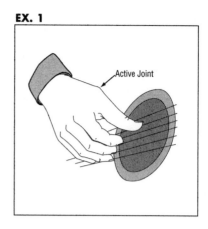

Active Joint

The illustration in **Ex. 1** shows hand positioning. The hand should hang naturally, near the rear of the soundhole. Some players—especially folk-blues guitarists—prefer to anchor their picking hand by bracing the ring finger or little finger against the top of the guitar. But it's strongly recommended that you start out with the position shown in the illustration, because it's more versatile.

A minimal amount of playing tension is necessary, and it should be confined to the hand. The wrist and arm should be relaxed. When plucking the strings, finger motion should be initiated at the knuckle, and thumb motion at the "active joint," as shown in Ex. 1. That ensures a stronger tone and more accurate stroke.

Now let's try a basic arpeggio, which is the sequential playing of the notes in a chord. The notation in **Ex. 2** has been simplified into "pattern-picking tablature." As in other tablatures, the lines represent the strings, with the lowest-sounding (sixth) on the lowest line, and the highest-sounding (first) on the highest line. We've used X's to indicate which strings to pick. Fret numbers aren't needed, because you will be playing only simple chords to learn the pattern, and the X's make it easier to visualize the sequence of the pattern.

In Ex. 2, the thumb (indicated by p) plays the bass note, the index finger (i) plays the third string, the middle finger (m) plays the second string, and the ring finger (a) plays the first string.

EX. 2

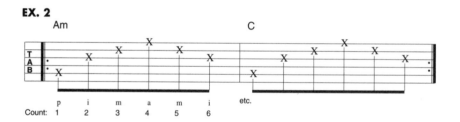

In all fingerpicking styles, the thumb is used almost exclusively for playing bass notes, and you can immediately add variety to a pattern by taking advantage of the bass notes available in the chords. Don't change the pattern in the treble (higher-sounding) strings, but pay attention to the way the bass note moves from string to string as you play the chords to "House of the Rising Sun," shown in **Ex. 3**. The bass line creates a feeling of movement and progression from chord to chord. Remember to keep the treble notes and rhythm constant throughout the song.

EX. 3

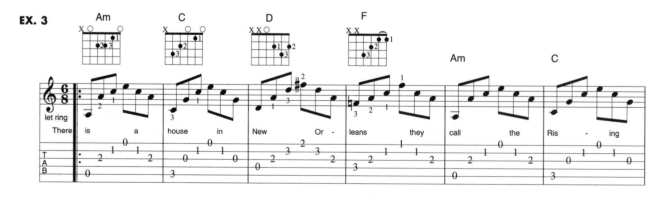

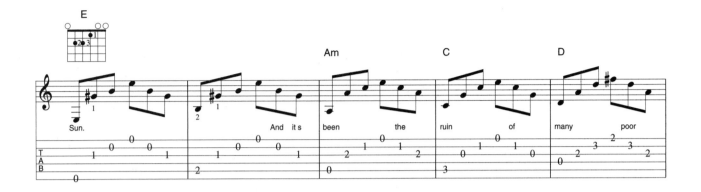

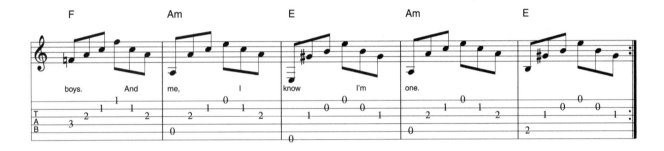

RAGTIME AND BLUES PICKING

The idea behind the ragtime and blues fingerpicking technique is simple. A steady rhythm is set up by the right-hand thumb as it picks down on one or more bass notes. That bass rhythm becomes the accompaniment for the melody, which is played on the treble strings with the index and middle fingers. The right-hand ring finger sometimes picks melody notes.

The bass may be played on one string (**Ex. 4**), on alternate strings (**Ex. 5**), or may be alternated between a single bass note and a chord (**Ex. 6**). These examples use regular, not pattern-picking, tablature.

The treble melody is played either *on* the beat (with the bass note), or *off* the beat (between the bass notes). Those off-beat notes are *syncopated*, and it's that syncopation that gives this fingerpicking style its distinctive, swinging sound.

However, syncopation is also the hardest thing for a beginning fingerpicker to get a handle on. The difficulty is in keeping the bass steady while the fingers play around the beat. Like rubbing your head while patting your belly, it takes practice to get it coordinated.

EX. 4   **EX. 5**   **EX. 6**

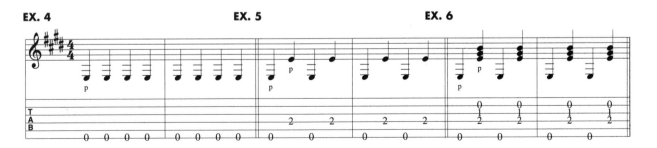

Examples 7a through **7e** show exercises you can do to get your fingers cooperating. First, fret an *E* chord and set up an alternating bass. Next, use your right-hand index finger to pick the second string, and use your middle finger to pick the first string as you play the exercise. Keep the alternating bass very steady.

All the treble notes in this set of exercises are *on* the beat, so they are played simultaneously with the thumb and the appropriate finger.

EX. 7a   **EX. 7b**

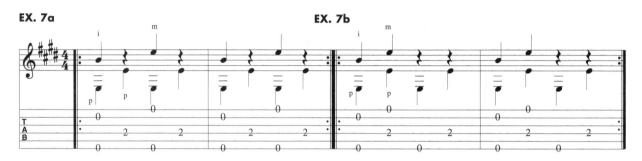

EX. 7c   **EX. 7d**   **EX. 7e**

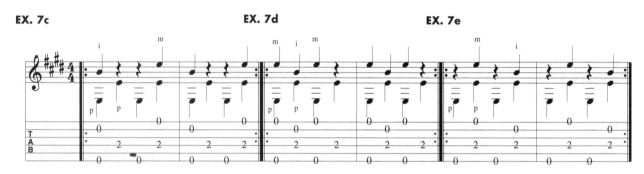

Ex. 8 shows a pattern you can build on to create an accompaniment plus melody. Try tapping your foot along with your thumb rhythm to keep the beat steady. By adding a note on the second string at the 2nd fret, you can play the first two lines of the song "John Henry." Everything in the treble is still squarely on the beat, right along with your thumb (**Ex. 9**).

EX. 8

If you take some of those melody notes and shift them ahead by one-half beat—putting them between the bass notes—you are syncopating the melody. **Ex. 10** presents an arrangement of "John Henry" with that kind of syncopation. When playing this example, make sure your thumb doesn't jump ahead with the treble notes. This takes some concentration, but with practice you'll master the rhythm and have the essence of fingerpicking. Play the arrangement slowly at first, and after you feel comfortable with it, try to work in your own syncopations. ■

EX. 9

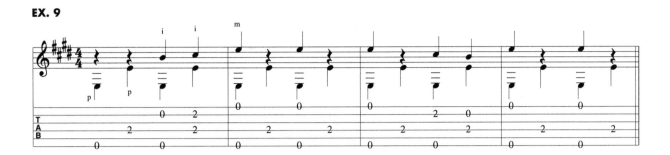

EX. 10

Blues on Target
THE ABC'S OF I–IV–V

BY ANDY ELLIS

Ever ask another guitarist how to solo over a I-IV-V blues progression? Nine times out of ten, you'll be admonished to practice a minor-pentatonic "box" scale. Chances are you already know one or more of these patterns—after all, most books, videos, and instructional tapes take this tack. But you can run blues scales until your fingers bleed, and you still won't sound righteous. Why?

B.B. King doesn't play scales. Albert King didn't either. Neither does Otis Rush, Hubert Sumlin, John Lee Hooker, Ry Cooder, or your local blues hero. Listen carefully to their music, and you'll hear the secret: It's *intervals*, not scale patterns, that make the magic happen. Blues vets work the space between notes, weaving in and out of the I-IV-V harmony. The concept is stunningly simple—a non-chord-tone creates tension, a chord-tone releases it—but infinitely deep.

Once you learn to hear and think in terms of harmonic color, you'll experience a radical transformation. Instead of meandering through scale patterns, wondering why your leads sound superficial and unfocused, you'll find yourself deep in the blues pocket. All that's required is a fresh perspective and a desire to explore chordal harmony.

Hubert Sumlin photo by Lisa Sharken

TRACK 8–11

In this lesson, we'll identify the killer chord-tones and learn how to move into and away from them with style. We'll play out of some fretboard positions that aren't obvious within scale patterns, yet are revealed by chord forms.

To help you visualize these new fingerings, we've kept all the examples in the key of A. This allows you to thoroughly absorb and map the interlocking moves before transposing them to other keys—something you must do gradually and persistently. We've also written this lesson's examples in 12/8. An easy time signature to read, it automatically provides a swinging three-within-four blues feel. Once you get into a key-of-A, 12/8 groove, you're there for the entire lesson.

These licks contain a wealth of information, much of which we discuss, but some of which is left for you to discover on your own. For maximum musical pay-off, listen to all examples against their respective chord changes.

In blues, the I, IV, and V are virtually always dominant chords. Whether played as 7th, 9th, or 13th voicings, a dominant chord contains an interval called the *tritone* (see FYI sidebar). Consisting of the 3rd and ♭7th degrees, the tritone defines the dominant sound. The 3 establishes the chord as major (as opposed to minor), and the ♭7 supplies its characteristic bite. Targeting tritones is a time-honored blues and R&B technique.

Ex. 1 comprises two classic tritone licks—first to *A7* (the I7), then *D7* (the IV7). Notice how *D7*'s tritone (*F♯-C♮*) lies a half-step below *A7*'s tritone (*G♮-C♯*). Same fingering and strings. Cool, huh? That ain't all: In that one-fret shift, the notes reverse roles—*A7*'s ♭7-3 becomes *D7*'s 3-♭7. Wait, there's more: *E7*'s tritone—*G♯-D♮*, or 3-♭7—lies a half-step above *A7*'s. There's a formula here: From the I7's tritone, simply move down a fret for the IV7 or up a fret for the V7. (This drama repeats itself six frets higher—hey, that's three whole-steps—on the same strings, only this time *A7*'s tritone is the 3-♭7 type and *D7*'s and *E7*'s are ♭7-3 babies.)

B.B. King popularized the chordal "rake" shown in **Ex. 2**. Five of the six subsequent notes are *Am7* chord-tones. This minor-melody-against-major-harmony sound is the essence of blues. Notice how the arpeggio leads smoothly to *E9*'s root, nailing the change. It's a Bluesbreaker lick: Eric Clapton, Peter Green, and Mick Taylor each worked variations on it.

Ex. 1

Ex. 2

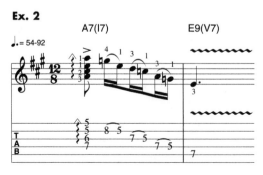

With minor adjustments, you can often tailor a lick to more than one chord. For example, graft a classic *Am7*-derived lick to *A7*, *D7*, and *E7* by targeting key chord-tones, as in **Ex. 3a** through **3c**. The lick resolves to *A7*'s root (Ex. 3a), *D7*'s 3rd (Ex. 3b), and *E7*'s 3rd (Ex. 3c), respectively. Pull the quarter-bend toward your feet.

It's helpful to learn three-note dominant-chord voicings all over the fretboard and use them as focal points for developing melodic lines. Practice the *E7*, *D7*, and *A7* shapes in **Ex. 4**, and then try **Ex. 5**, a V7-IV7-I7 phrase. See how each chord shape is incorporated into its corresponding lick? The *D7* grip (bar 2, beats *one* and *two*) is particularly gnarly—Robert Johnson all the way. That last interval jump in bar 2 is a nifty tritone shape.

Ex. 3a

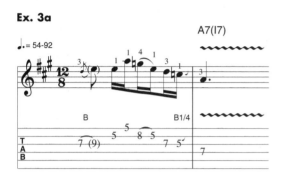

Ex. 3b

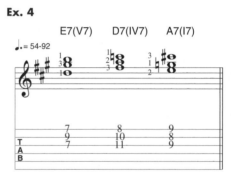

Ex. 3c

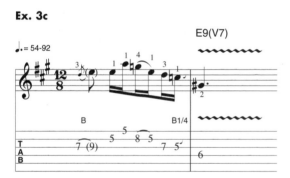

Ex. 4

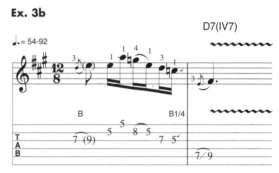

Ex. 5

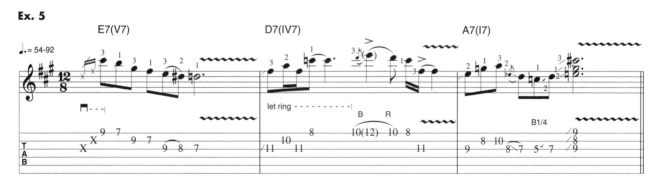

TRITONE TWINS

AND THE
FLAT-FIVE SUBSTITUTION

The tritone—an interval of three whole-steps, or a diminished fifth—divides an octave in half. Inverted, this symmetrical interval remains a tritone. In a dominant 7th chord, the 3rd and ♭7th degrees form a tritone. For example, *E7*'s tritone is *G#-D*. Invert this, and you get *D-G#* (*A♭*), the 3rd and ♭7th of *B♭7*. Since *E7* and *B♭7* are tritone twins, you can substitute one for the other. You can swap *any* two dominants (whether dominant 7th, 9th, or 13th chords) whose roots are a diminished fifth apart. This "flat-five substitution" is a jazz mainstay. ■

Ex. 6a and **Ex. 6b** present another "same lick, different application" scenario. The tags are *A7* and *D7* tritones, played this time on the fifth and fourth strings. In the key of *A*, map out the I7-IV7-V7 tritones on these strings, in both 3-♭7 and ♭7-3 configurations. Mastering tritones, especially on the inside four strings, will ratchet your playing to the next level.

Skipping strings—a handy death-to-scales tactic—gives your leads compelling contours. In **Ex. 7**, slam *E9* and *D9* with a favorite Albert King/Stevie Ray wide-interval move that *feels* as groovy as it sounds. Bar 2 oozes non-box-scale thinking as well. Note the diminished fifth (*E♭-A*) followed by the sly half-step slide. By contrasting large and small intervals, you maintain melodic interest.

Scale-pattern adherents would see **Ex. 8** as a run that traverses second- and fifth-position boxes. But that wouldn't do justice to the *colors* you're generating. Try another view: In bar 1, while flirting with the minor/major axis, you're dancing with an *Amaj6* arpeggio (*A-C#-E-F#*) and letting it lead you up the neck. In bar 2, you're moving in and out of *D9*, skipping strings along the way and shifting positions to accommodate the flowing melody.

Here's another very interval-oriented strategy: Work a chromatic line against a stationary note, as in **Ex. 9**, a traditional blues turnaround. How about that *Eaug* at the end? Whammy it up—whew!

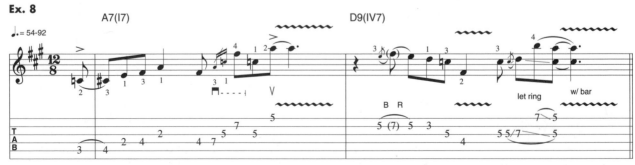

Ex. 9

12-BAR BASICS

There are 16-bar and eight-bar blues forms, but by far the most popular is the 12-bar scheme. A basic blues progression consists of the I, IV, and V chords of a key—played as dominant voicings—stretched across 12 bars as shown in **Fig. 1a**. Another popular form, called the "quick change," breaks up that initial four-bar I7 stretch (**Fig. 1b**).

Determining what the I, IV, and V chords are in any given key is a snap using the cycle of fourths/fifths chart (**Fig. 2**). Here's how to do it:

• Choose your key.

• From that note, move one note counterclockwise for the IV chord and one letter clockwise for the V.

• Make the three chords dominant—use either 7th, 9th, or 13th voicings—and you're done.

For example, let's find the three chords in, say, the key of B♭. From B♭, one counterclockwise move yields E♭ (the IV), and one clockwise move produces F (the V). The I7, IV7, and V7 chords in B♭ are B♭7, E♭7, and F7.

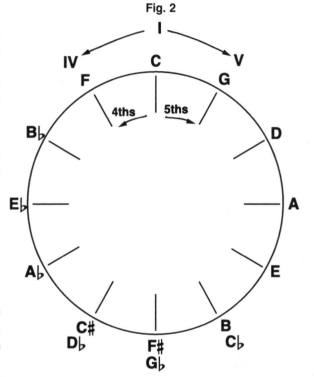

You can practice the 12-bar blues progression by playing along with the rhythm tracks on the CD. There are three basic blues rhythm tracks, featuring progressions in *F*, in *C*, and in *E*. These allow you to work on simple chord changes, or tip-toe into the area of improvisation.

"Blues Progression in *F*" (track 9) has a chugging rock 'n' roll feel with a splash of honky-tonk piano. "Blues Progression in *C*" (track 10) is a sultry slow blues that gives you plenty of room for stretching out or comping, whatever your pleasure. It's got a "Stormy Monday" kind of vibe. You'll get to dig into some cool turnarounds. "Blues Progression in *E*" (track 11) is a spirited shuffle. This one revs right along, swinging heartily, and features some cool stops that will create some open spaces for you.   ■

Fig. 1												
bar number:	1	2	3	4	5	6	7	8	9	10	11	12
(a) basic 12-bar:	I7	/	/	/	IV7	/	I7	/	V7	IV7	I7	V7
(b) quick change:	I7	IV7	I7	/	IV7	/	I7	/	V7	IV7	I7	V7

Ten of the 11 notes in **Ex. 10** are *D9* chord-tones, yet the lick is melodic and bluesy. There's no mistaking what chord you're orbiting. That's good, since in the real world, an audience doesn't take kindly to bandstand meandering.

Arpeggio city: The lick in **Ex. 11**, with its twists, turns, slides, and bends, is unpredictable and decidedly non-scalar. The last five notes—skipped-strings alert—are utterly Jimi. Watch the fingering.

By now **Ex. 12**'s ingredients should be familiar: Arpeggio-based melodies, greasy slides, pull-offs, minor/major teases—all topped with a vibratoed tritone. Hit the bend in bar 2 hard—you want the note to sing through the release.

There are two slick position shifts in **Ex. 13**. Both figures start at the 8th fret and move to the 10th to oblige a hammer/pull fest. When you release that last bend, make sure *C* sustains against the subsequent *F♯* to create a tritone. With the right power-tube distortion, this interval wails like a banshee.

More shades o' Jimi in **Ex. 14**. He took the hammered double-stop action in beat four, previously considered a country move, and made it an essential blues-rock figure. It rubs sensually against the *E9*, don't you think? (Hendrix hung out in Nashville for a while, and it shows in "The Wind Cries Mary.")

Watch the position shift in **Ex. 15** (bar 1, beat four). This lick winds up in SRV turf. For a hip, late-'50s Blue Note sound, *à la* Kenny Burrell and Grant Green, play

Ex. 10

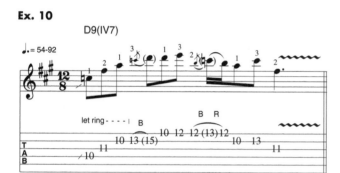

Ex. 11

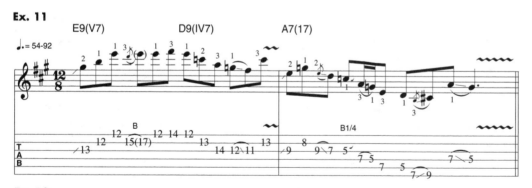

Ex. 12

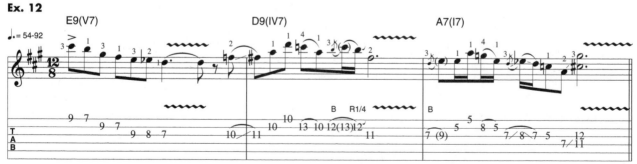

bar 1's I7 double-stop routine over the IV7 and V7. Simply transpose the action so you hit the chord-of-the-moment's tritone with that last slide.

Ex. 16 features a chromatic opening, beaucoup sliding sixths, and Hendrixy double-stops. Ending at the fifth position, the lick migrates from the eighth through the fourth positions. It's fluid, melodic, and bears scant connection to scale patterns.

Ex. 13

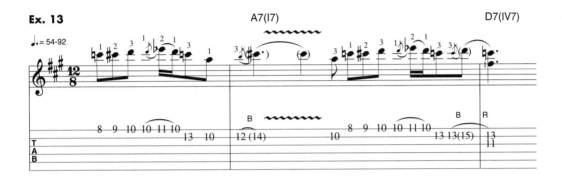

Ex. 14

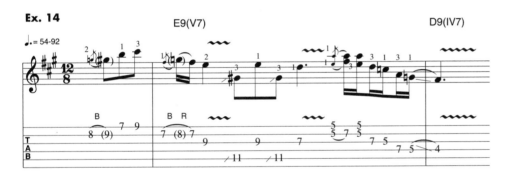

Ex. 15

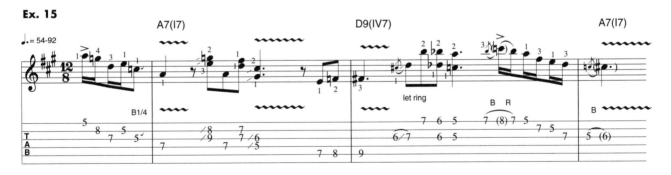

Ex. 16

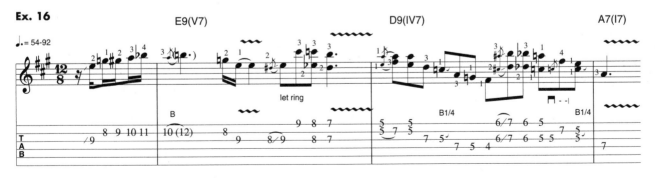

To explore chord-targeting concepts on your own, remember these guidelines:

- Revisit all the chords you know, listening to them one or two notes at a time (remember to audition the widest available intervals). With a clear picture of the fretboard shape in your mind, move into each chord-tone from above and below. Try approaching chord-tones from a half-step below and either a half- or a whole-step above. Then jump to them from a string or two away. Reverse the process, moving from chord-tones to other notes. When you find an intriguing way to outline a chord melodically, tie the move to your favorite licks.

- As you discover how to outline individual chords, start practicing over progressions, linking one sketch smoothly to the next.

- When you learn a new chord, don't stop with the static grip. Take time to explore single- and double-note approaches and exits to the harmony.

- Brush up on chord theory. Learn how the four basic chord types are constructed (major, minor, augmented, diminished) and how to convert these triads into seventh chords, extended chords, and altered chords.

- Sing along with your lines. It's another magic bullet that enhances your melodic sensibilities while subverting the dreaded scale syndrome.

- Develop your interval awareness by listening to great blues players of all eras. As guitarists, we can learn a lot from harp and sax players, because they don't have to contend with box patterns.

- Above all, learn to follow your ears, not your fingers. ■

Barre Chords and Beyond

GAIN WITHOUT PAIN

BY ARLEN ROTH

To many guitar players the very mention of barre chords sends them running, mainly from the painful memories of learning these fretboard necessities. Well, I've got refreshing news for all you beginners: *It's not that bad!* One of the main misconceptions about barre chords is that you need to press down all the strings that the barreing finger is covering. This is simply not so, and a lot of the pain we associate with these chord forms is not only because of this fact, but also that the wrong part of the finger is involved.

Arlen Roth and Duane Eddy
photo courtesy of Hot Licks Productions, Inc.

Let's start with the basics. First, it's important to understand that barre chords enable us to move normally open chord positions, most notably *A* and *E* forms, up to uncharted territory. The barred notes are those we previously played as open strings, only now the barre acts as a replacement for the guitar's nut. **Ex. 1** (next page) shows how the *E*-form barre chord looks when you move it up to play an *F* chord at the first fret.

TRACK 12

EX. 1

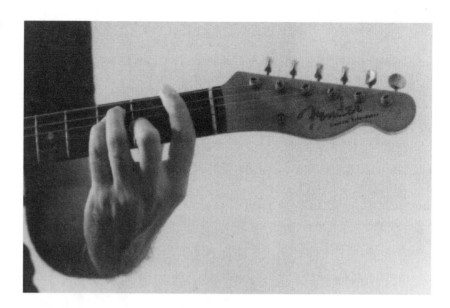

An important thing to note about the picture and my hand position is how I'm using the side (bony) part of the index finger to create the barre. You should also note that this creates a curved look to the position, which is much more desirable than a flat position in which you simply press down on the underside (fleshy) part of the finger, which usually results in a lot more pain. The other important aspect of these positions is that you only need to sound the low E, the B, and the high E strings with the barre. Since the other fingers are covering the notes of the chord, much of the burden is relieved from the barreing finger, so it can curl around nicely and just catch the notes on the first, second, and sixth strings. That's why barre chords can look more formidable than they actually are.

Ex. 2 shows the A-form barre chords moved up to a closed position. The chord is now a $B\flat$ at the 1st fret. This time, note how the index finger only has to cover *five* strings and the barred notes are simply on the A string and the high E string. Once again, the curl of the index finger, and the fact that we're using the bony side, help cover these notes fairly painlessly.

EX. 2

ARPEGGIATING BARRE CHORDS

Though barre chords can often seem a bit static and cumbersome, one of the more lyrical techniques we can use is the arpeggio, which is when we play the notes in a chord singly, in a series. Guitar arpeggios are often heard in old rhythm-and-blues songs, such as those played by Steve Cropper with Otis Redding, Wilson Pickett, and Sam and Dave. The style can be extremely effective for a rhythm or lead guitar part. In many of these types of licks, sliding into the beginning of the first note of the arpeggio creates a kind of tension that produces a nice effect. **Ex. 3** is a simple progression in the key of *G* that uses three kinds of positions: the *E*-form barre chord, the open *E* minor chord, and the *A*-form barre chord for both the *C* and *D* chords. Use the opening slides to give the licks a more "true to life" effect, and play the progression slowly with a nice even tempo.

EX. 3

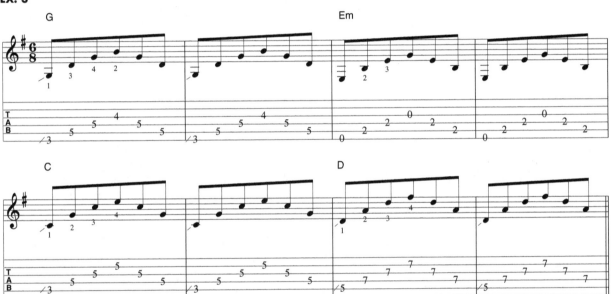

PARTIAL BARRES AS SLIDES

This technique is another R&B-based sound that's simple in structure but highly effective when used with rhythm guitar arpeggios. Partial-barre "slide" licks, as I like to call them, are played almost exclusively with the index finger, barreing the top two strings. In this barre, it helps to use a slightly flatter position, compared with the technique I recommended for the full-chord positions. **Ex. 4** shows a few basic slide licks you can practice. Make the slides smooth, avoiding jumpy or erratic motion by the barre as it moves from fret to fret.

EX. 4

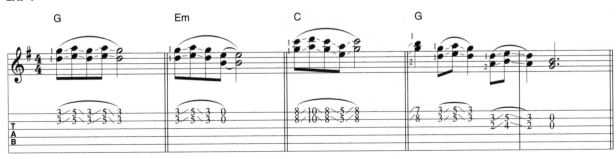

PUTTING IT ALL TOGETHER

When you get these two new techniques under your belt, try them out on a real piece of music. The tune I've written in **Ex. 5** is based on the soulful ballads of the early Memphis Stax/Volt sound, and it shows how that in guitar playing, less is often truly more. I've combined the barre-chord arpeggios with the index-finger barre slides as transitions between chord changes or measures, so you can see how these take on a melodic quality. You'll probably have a little trouble at first moving from one position to another, so proceed slowly and carefully until your confidence builds and you can really make it sing. Feel free to experiment with the ideas I've given you, using different chord progressions and slide positions. I think you'll be pleasantly surprised at what you come up with. ■

EX. 5

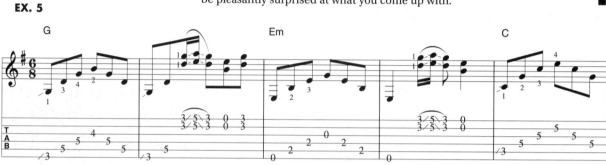

Musician, Hear Thyself

HONING YOUR PERFORMANCES THROUGH SMART PRACTICE

BY HOWARD MORGEN

Listening critically and objectively to oneself while singing or playing is difficult, if not impossible, for most musicians. Singers have a particularly hard time because the sound heard in the head is not the sound heard by the audience. It's a little easier for instrumentalists, because the sound is produced outside the body, but the concentration most instruments require can make it difficult for a performer to hear the big picture. This is certainly true for guitarists, who deal with multi-voiced music. It's easy to believe you are clearly "hearing" notes that in fact aren't being articulated cleanly—or aren't being sounded at all.

Tom Dumont of No Doubt photo by John Popplewell

Hour after hour of well-intentioned practicing is often wasted on unfocused repetition of error and correction in the hope that everything will eventually come together. But until a player can, through careful, attentive listening, take control of each element that goes into a good performance, real command of the material is unlikely. Simply put, if you can't hear where the problem is, you can't fix it.

One way out of this conundrum is to have a good teacher, one who will act as that essential extra set of ears. That teacher, however, will seldom be there when you practice. The best method to get the feedback you need is to religiously record your playing.

While most of us use recorders for transferring music, taping concerts, and copping licks, few incorporate recordings as an integral part of the daily practice routine. For many, once that recorder is activated, the stress factor takes over and the mistakes begin to multiply. It's unpleasant to hear a piece unravel after you think you've "nailed" it. At those times, listening can be downright painful to the ego. That's the bad news. The good news is that if you can accept and even welcome those unsettling feelings as dues you must pay for real and permanent progress, the discomfort can be used to your advantage.

First, it's normal to feel increased stress and scattered concentration during a live performance, so it helps to train yourself to function under that kind of pressure. Think of the recorder as your audience. Second, you should uncover as many potential trouble spots as possible *before* a performance. So the more "clams" you hit because of nerves during practice, the better prepared you'll be on stage.

You'll be surprised how quickly your performances will start to shape up if you focus first on the parts that displease you the most, and then find ways to fix them. Just be patient with yourself, and don't try to record "perfect takes" at first. Remember, you're the only one who is going to hear those early efforts.

Be prepared to record and listen many times, so you can work with as many aspects of your performance as possible. You can't possibly hear all the nuances of tone, dynamics, phrasing, interpretation, technique, tempo, etc., in one playback.

It's a good idea to use a metronome or drum machine while recording, to help you find tempos that feel "in the pocket." But it's also informative—and humbling—to record while relying only on your own sense of time, to find situations in which you are likely to rush or drag.

It won't take long for you to realize the value of consistent self-appraisal. You'll probably accomplish more in one day of this kind of intense, recorded workout than you would in weeks of second-guessing and wishful thinking. ∎

GUITAR BONDING: AN INSPIRATIONAL DISCOGRAPHY

One of the most direct routes to musical inspiration is through the works of the masters. With that in mind, we've assembled this discography to give you a small sample of great playing in a number of styles. We hope you'll use it not only to find albums by your favorites, but also to discover unfamiliar guitarists. Whether it's a lick, a tone, or an emotion, all of these players have something to teach you.

ROCK

The Ventures
Walk—Don't Run: The Best of the Ventures
[EMI]

Jimi Hendrix
Axis Bold as Love
[MCA]

Cream (Eric Clapton)
Wheels of Fire
[Polydon]

Van Halen (Eddie Van Halen)
Van Halen
[Warner Bros.]

Jeff Beck
Blow by Blow
[Epic]

Led Zeppelin
(Jimmy Page)
Led Zeppelin [Atlantic]

Eric Johnson
Tones
[Reprise]

Steve Vai
Passion & Warfare
[Relativity]

BLUES

Joe Satriani
Surfing with the Alien
[Sony/Epic]

B.B. King
Live at the Regal
[MCA]

Robert Johnson
The Complete Recordings
[Sony/Columbia]

Stevie Ray Vaughan
In Step
[Sony/Columbia]

JAZZ

Albert King
King of the Blues Guitar
[Atlantic]

John Mayall
Blues Breakers with Eric Clapton
[Deram]

Charlie Christian
The Genius of the Electric Guitar
[Columbia]

Django Reinhardt
*Peche à la Mouche—
The Great Blue Star Sessions*
[Verve]

Les Paul
The Best of the Capitol Masters
[Capitol]

Wes Montgomery
The Artistry of Wes Montgomery
[Riverside]

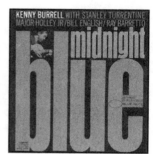

Kenny Burrell
Midnight Blue
[Blue Note]

Joe Pass
Virtuoso
[Pablo]

COUNTRY/BLUEGRASS/FOLK

Miles Davis (John Scofield, Mike Stern)
Star People
[Sony]

Mahavishnu Orchestra
(John McLaughlin)
Birds of Fire [Columbia/Legacy]

Chet Atkins
The RCA Years
[RCA]

Leo Kottke
6- & 12-String Guitar
[Takoma]

Doc Watson
Doc Watson
[Vanguard]

Tony Rice
Tony Rice
[Rounder]

Vince Gill
High Lonesome Sound
[MCA]

Brent Mason
Hot Wired
[Polygram]

CLASSICAL/NEW ACOUSTIC

Andres Segovia
The Segovia Collection (Vol. 1): Bach
[MCA Classics]

Julian Bream and John Williams
Together
[RCA]

Michael Hedges
Aerial Boundaries
[Windham Hill]

Badi Assad
Solo
[Chesky]

hart
A GUITAR

an
these
he
itar's
nd

photo by Paul Haggard

A straight neck is a must. To check this, hold the guitar by its neck and body, and sight it down from the headstock end (**Ex. 1**, next page). Make sure the guitar is equipped with a truss rod. If the neck isn't straight, the strings might buzz. Loosening the truss rod's adjusting nut creates an upward arc, or "relief," that can eliminate buzzing. It's best if the truss rod also has the ability to "back-bow" the neck, so that in years to come it may be adjusted in that direction if the string pull causes the neck to have too much "up-bow." Ask a salesman or in-store repair person to demonstrate this adjustment. In the past, inexpensive guitars often had either poorly working rods or none at all. Now, most guitars—even inexpensive imports—have effective truss rods, but make sure for yourself before you buy.

ACOUSTIC

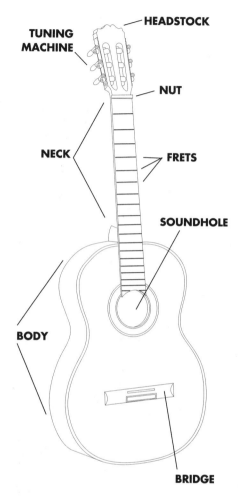

TUNING
MACHINE

HEADSTOCK

NUT

NECK

FRETS

SOUNDHOLE

BODY

BRIDGE

FRETS

It wasn't too long ago that the only good fret jobs were on big-name, American-made guitars. Not so anymore. These days, even low-end models have well-installed high-quality fret wire. Look to see that the frets are seated well against the fingerboard, especially checking the fret ends for looseness or jagged edges (the telltale signs of a poorly made guitar). Check the frets all the way up the fingerboard. Press with your thumbnail to see if there is any give between the fret and fingerboard.

FINGERBOARD WOOD

What wood is the fingerboard made of? Most guitars come with hardwood fingerboards: ebony, rosewood, or maple. Avoid guitars with mahogany or plywood fingerboards that have been stained black or reddish-brown to look like the real thing. If you shop in a large store with a wide selection, you often find two guitars that seem the same, yet are $50 to $100 apart in price. Check the fingerboard. One may have high-quality wood with real pearl inlays instead of plastic; the more expensive one is worth the extra money.

ACTION

Test the guitar's playability, or "action." This is mostly determined by the nut and bridge. Don't expect the string height at the nut to be perfect on any new guitar, since it is left slightly tall at the factory to accommodate different players' tastes. These final adjustments are usually done by repair people at the store before or after the sale. Adjusting the bridge saddle height is easy on most electrics, but difficult with acoustics. With acoustics, look for a combination of a saddle that's approximately 1/8" or slightly more above the bridge top, and an easy string height. This means that strings can be pressed to the fingerboard without too much effort (**Examples 2** and **3**). Adequate height creates a strong angle where the string passes over the saddle, and increases the chance for good volume and tone. Avoid acoustics with low saddles, unless the strings are also low on the fingerboard, allowing the action to be comfortable when the saddle is raised or replaced. With any guitar, be sure that the saddle or bridge allows you to play in tune when you depress any string at the 12th fret. Listen for notes that are out of tune. If the guitar cannot be adjusted quickly by a competent repair person, look at something else. (For advice on setting up your guitar yourself, see page 10.)

EX. 1

EX. 2

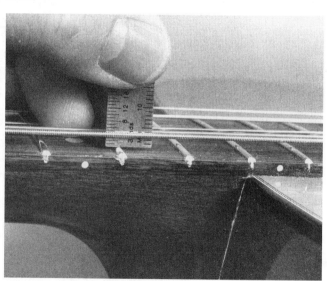

photos by Nora Sturges

TUNERS

Tuning machines are always important, but these days most guitars come with good tuners. (We repairmen used to make a lot of money installing Grovers a few years back, but times have changed.) You're pretty safe with any tuners you buy now.

BRACES

When buying an acoustic, take along an inspection mirror to look inside the guitar. Search for sloppy glue jobs and especially for loose bracing under the bridge area. Any decent lighting will help your mirror show you the insides (**Ex. 4**). A loose brace may appear as a dark line between the brace and what it's bracing. If you're in doubt, loosen the strings, reach inside, and hold the brace with your fingers while gently pressing from the outside. If a brace is loose, you'll feel movement there. Look for clean work, remembering that the more you spend, the better the ax should look.

PICKUPS

If you're shopping for an electric guitar, make note of the difference between active and passive pickup systems. At one time, the vast majority of pickups were passive, but now many manufacturers offer active systems. These low-impedance pickups run off of a 9-volt battery and can offer hum-free signals. This means a cleaner sound, even at high volume. If you want a wide range of sounds, active pickups should appeal to you. While active electronics once were a luxury item used only by the most discriminating professionals, now anyone can buy these systems on stock guitars at affordable prices. Check them out.

FINISH

Finally, check the finish. Look for binding that has been scraped clean of any color, and note defects or scratches. I've been impressed by the flatness—the lack of ripples—and buffing jobs on even the lowest-end guitars. Never buy a guitar on its looks alone though. By carefully examining your potential purchase, you greatly improve your chances of avoiding the dreaded lemon. ■

ELECTRIC

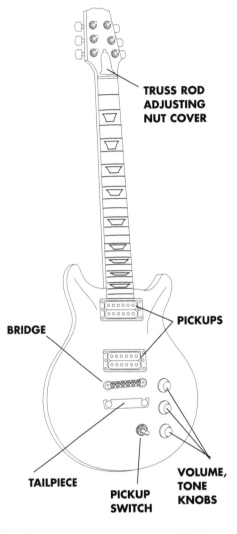

TRUSS ROD ADJUSTING NUT COVER

BRIDGE

PICKUPS

TAILPIECE

PICKUP SWITCH

VOLUME, TONE KNOBS

EX. 3

EX. 4

A BASIC GUITAR GLOSSARY

Here's a list of terms that will give you clout in the music store, as well as help you understand your own ax. Cross-referenced words are in bold type.

• •

Action. The **strings**' playability along the **neck**. Action is affected by the strings' distance from the neck, the neck straightness, and string gauge.

Acoustic. A hollow**body** guitar that does not require electronic amplification.

Archtop. A guitar, often an **acoustic**, with a curved top (**soundboard**) and *f*-**holes** similar to a violin's.

Binding. Thin strips of wood or plastic that seal the edges of the **body**.

Body. The main part of the guitar, to which the **bridge** and **neck** are attached. On acoustic guitars and some electrics, the body serves as a resonating chamber.

Braces. Interior wooden strips that strengthen a hollowbody guitar. Brace size and configuration partly determine a guitar's tone.

Bridge. The structure that holds the **saddle** (or saddles), over which **strings** pass on the guitar body. Most bridges can be adjusted to raise or lower string height, changing the guitar's **action** and intonation.

Cutaway. An indented area of the body that allows the guitarist's fretting hand to access notes higher up the neck.

Electric. A guitar that requires amplification in order to be heard properly.

f-**holes.** Violin-style v-shaped **soundholes**, usually found in pairs.

Flat-top. A guitar whose **soundboard**, or top, is flat.

Fretboard. The wooden strip, usually of hardwood, attached atop the **neck** and into which the **frets** are set. Also called the fingerboard.

Frets. Metal wires set into the fretboard at precise distances, allowing the strings to sound the correct pitches along the neck.

Headstock. The structure at the end of the **neck** that holds the tuning machines.

Neck. The long structure that runs from the **body** to the **headstock**, and onto which the **fretboard** is attached. Necks have a longitudinal curve that can be adjusted by means of the **truss rod**. The width, shape, and curvature of the neck largely determine a guitar's playability.

Nut. The notched fitting—usually of bone, ivory, ebony, metal, or plastic—that guides the strings from the **fretboard** to the **tuning machines**.

Pickguard. A piece of flat plastic that protects the top from being scratched by a pick or fingers.

Pickup. The device that senses the **strings**' vibrations and converts them into electric impulses that can be amplified. Most **electrics** have from one to three pickups. Most pickups are electromagnetic, though piezoelectric pickups are also used.

Pickup switch. Allows pickups to be turned on individually or in various combinations.

Potentiometer (pot). A variable resistor used for an electric guitar's volume and tone controls. Amplifiers also have pots.

Saddle. The fitting that guides the **strings** over the **bridge**. Most **electric** guitars have individual saddles for each string. These can be adjusted to change a **string's** length and thus intonation.

Solidbody. A guitar whose **body** is made from a solid piece of wood or is a solid lamination. Most electrics are solidbodies; some are semi-hollow.

Soundboard. The resonating top of an acoustic guitar.

Soundhole. A hole (or holes) in the top of a guitar through which sound is emitted.

Strings. The cords that are plucked to cause vibrations that produce a guitar's sound. Most guitar strings are solid wire or thin wire wrapped around a solid core; classical guitars have nylon and metal-wound nylon strings. A string's thickness (gauge) depends on its position on the guitar and the relative thickness of the entire 6-string set.

Tailpiece. The device that holds the strings' ball-ends.

Tuning machines. Devices set into the **headstock** that anchor **strings** and allow them to be tuned. Each tuning machine consists of a post, a geared mechanism, and a tuning key.

Truss rod. A metal rod that runs lengthwise through the **neck**, increasing its strength and allowing adjustment of the longitudinal curve.

Truss rod adjusting nut. The part of the **truss rod** system that can be tightened or loosened to alter rod tension, in turn changing the **neck** curvature.   ■

Knowledge Is Power

How to Buy an Amp

BY ED SCHILLING & TERRY BUDDINGH

Choosing the amp that's right for you may seem like a daunting task, considering the multitude of choices available today. But you can reduce your option anxiety considerably by first identifying your needs. Then you can begin your search among the amps that fulfill those requirements.

Only you can decide what features and price range suit you the best. And remember: There wouldn't be so many choices if there weren't so many people looking for so many different features and sounds from their amps.

Dimebag Darrell photo by Lisa Sharken

THINKING AHEAD

A few key factors will determine your amp choice: Its primary function—practice, performing, or recording; your musical style; the amp configurations available; and how much money you want to spend.

Function. Practice amps should give you an acceptable sound at a volume that won't get you evicted. Elaborate tone and effects controls are not as important; your goal is to practice notes, not electronics.

Performance amps, on the other hand, must deliver every aspect of your sound—proper gain, tone equalization (EQ), effects, and volume—with quick and easy adjustments.

You can use any amp for recording sessions, providing it doesn't generate a lot of background noise. But small, high-quality amps are often preferred for recording, since you can push them to their limits at more reasonable volumes than you can larger stage amps. A skilled recording engineer can make a small amp sound huge.

Does this mean that you need three amps? Not at all. A well-chosen combo amp (a one-piece system, with amp, tone controls, and speakers in the same box) can work admirably in all three situations.

Musical style. Your style should help determine your amp choice. For example, if you play folk or country music with electrified acoustic guitars, you need a good EQ section and full-range speakers, not a raging 100-watt tube amp with potentially lethal overdrive. Jazz, too, often calls for a good clean tone, not hair-raising distortion.

Configuration. Combo amps are the most popular type, and they come in a wide array of sizes. Their features range from single-knob tone and volume controls to multi-channel circuitry with built-in digital effects and multi-band EQ. Acoustic, country, jazz, pop, and rock guitarists use combo amps with great success.

Most battery-powered, pocket-sized **headphone amps** don't have built-in speakers. They deliver full distortion at headphone volume and are adequate for practicing. You may be able to use them as outboard preamps with another amplifier. ("Outboard" refers to external signal-processing gear. Most guitar effects are outboard.)

Piggyback-style amps separate the amp's electronics from the speaker cabinet. Fender popularized the piggyback configuration in the '60s. The classic Marshall "stack," with a head perched atop two 4x12 cabinets, is probably the most recognizable piggyback amp. (The "4x12" refers to speaker configuration; in this case, the four 12" speakers in one cabinet.) The amp's electronics is called the "head," "top," or "brain."

Concert stacks, with separate amplifier heads and two (or more) large speaker cabinets, were designed for and made famous by high-volume rockers such as Pete Townsend and Jimi Hendrix. A half-stack is an amp and a single speaker enclosure (usually a 4x12).

Rackmount systems are popular with studio guitarists who want maximum control over their sound and are willing to pay for it. The player fills a standard 19.5"-wide rack enclosure with a separate preamp, amp, and whatever effects components suit his or her needs.

Price. How much will this shopping spree cost? Under $150 for a practice amp; up to $1,500 for most combos; $1,800 or $3,000 for concert stacks ($1,200 to $1,400 for a half-stack); and $2,500 to $5,000 for a well-equipped rackmount system.

FEATURES

Once you decide which configuration is best for you, it's time to test-drive a few amps at your local store. Here are some key features to look for:

Channels. Many manufacturers offer multi-channel amps that allow you to optimize each channel for different sounds—one for lead, another for crunch rhythm, another for clean rhythm, etc.—and change quickly among them by stomping on a footswitch.

Inputs. Some amps offer two inputs for each channel. The second input is typically designed to provide less gain for a cleaner sound.

Gain. The gain knob controls the amount of boost the preamp gives to an incoming signal. High gain-knob settings can overdrive the preamp, which produces sustain-enhancing distortion.

Equalization. Equalizers are tone controls. They shape a sound by boosting or cutting particular frequencies. There are three main types of EQs: 1. Wide-band-pass filters, which usually consist of individual knobs labeled "bass," "midrange" (or "mid"), and "treble." 2. Narrower-band graphic EQs, which use vertical sliders to adjust the relative volumes of preset frequencies. (The region each slider affects is called a "band"; the more bands an equalizer has, the more precise it is.) 3. Parametric EQs, which allow you to dial in exactly which frequencies are cut or boosted, as well as by what amount.

Graphic EQs are effective and easy to deal with, while parametric controls require more practice and skill.

Effects: The overwhelming popularity of digital effects has prompted some combo amp manufacturers to furnish built-in reverb, echo, flanging, and/or chorusing. Do you need them? More important, do you like the quality of the effects on a particular amp? If the answer is "yes" to both questions, great. What if the answer is "no"? Built-in effects may be convenient, but they're not for everybody. If you're particular about effects, your best choice may be an amp with an effects loop.

Effects loop. Consisting of merely input and output jacks for connecting outboard gear, this might seem like a non-feature. But these jacks allow you to connect your favorite effects devices somewhere other than between your guitar and amp input. This makes for a less noisy signal and a neater setup with fewer long cords. In addition, many loops are located after the amp's tone-shaping circuitry, allowing you to add, say, echo after your distortion and tone. Adjustable input and output level controls enable the effects loop to accept a wide range of effects. Outboard effects have variable input sensitivity and output strength, and the controls let you find just the right matching signal levels. If no such knobs are offered, look for an electronically buffered effects loop—it has circuitry that keeps mismatches between the amp and effects from degrading your signal.

Power. Stage amps need the most power, but the increasing sophistication of PA systems means that you might not need hundreds of watts to perform. Ask yourself, "What do I want onstage? Something to project my sound or simply provide an onstage monitor?" If you just need a monitor, mike a small amp, or take a direct line out, and your signal will go through the mixing board and out through the PA.

Even if you want to operate at maximum volume, you don't necessarily need a zillion-watt amp. Some high-wattage amps need to be opened up to deafening volume levels to get a vicious tone with long sustain. If you're practicing or recording, you might not be able to do that. For that reason, you might prefer a 50-watt amp to a 100-watt model. According to many tone connoisseurs, distortion quality is indeed affected by the amount of power available. Many say a lower wattage amp operated at high volume will tend to produce more output-tube distortion than preamp-tube distortion, producing a smoother and richer tone.

The most important thing to remember is that comparing different manufacturers' published power ratings is not always a reliable method of evaluating amps' differences. For one thing, some manufacturers' specs are more optimistic than others. And since it takes a doubling of power to increase volume by 3dB, quibbling over a few meaningless watts is unnecessary. The best advice? Choose an amp by listening in the store and onstage, not by comparing power ratings.

Speakers. For guitar, 12"-diameter speakers are the most common, followed by 10" and 15" speakers.

Different brands and models of speakers produce different sounds. For example, players who enjoy speaker breakup as part of their distortion favor speakers such as Celestion's popular Vintage 30- or 25-watt Greenbacks. Guitarists who seek more clarity and definition might opt for JBL or Electro-Voice speakers with higher power ratings, say 75 to 150 watts.

The enclosure is a big factor in amplified sound. A cleverly designed enclosure can, for instance, make a 10' speaker sound deeper than a 15". Also, the most efficient cabinet design in terms of sheer loudness might not produce the most desirable tone. For example, an open-backed speaker enclosure isn't very efficient, but many guitarists swear by their "open" and multi-dimensional sound.

Once you've selected an amp with the right features, perform a few tests: Check all the controls, and look for warning signs. Strum a chord and listen to the output. Is it pleasant, or harsh? Turn your guitar volume down, turn all the amp knobs to 10, and see how much residual noise there is. Some amps oscillate (squeal) at high-gain settings. As you're playing, reach over and rap the top of the amp with your fist to see if there are any vibration problems.

TUBE OR SOLID STATE?

Which is better: the warm, smooth tone of vacuum tubes or the sharp bite of solid state? Personal preferences aside, there are some technical points that may sway your decision.

"Valve (tube) amps will normally keep going in conditions that will destroy a transistor amp," says Jim Marshall, founder of Marshall Amplification. "With the high gain of today's amplifiers, it is very easy to achieve a state of instability, which means the amp delivers large amounts of power beyond its designed parameters. A valve amp can tolerate this condition for reasonable lengths of time without damage, but the same condition will destroy the output stage of a transistor amp very quickly." Normally, when a tube amp is heavily overdriven this way, the treble decreases, which helps produce the characteristic "fat" tube sound.

Solid-state amps usually have wider frequency ranges and offer a cleaner, clearer sound. They often provide greater EQ ranges as well. Tubes are more vulnerable to vibration and physical abuse. They get very hot, unlike transistors. For some players, the solution is to use a tube-powered pedal, effects unit, or preamp to drive a solid-state amp.

RACKMOUNT SYSTEMS

If your sound depends heavily on signal processing, a rack system will give you maximum flexibility. Most people start out with a programmable preamp (often tube-powered) and add their preferred effects, such as delay, chorus, echo, flanging, and reverb. A sophisticated equalizer, either graphic or parametric, provides tone control. You can also add compressor/limiters, noise reduction units, and maybe a small mixer. Many players choose stereo amps with several hundred watts per side.

USED AMPS

So you don't have $3,000 for a stack or a rack? Not to worry. You can get a good used amp for less than half of what you might pay for it new. But it usually won't have a warranty, so check the unit carefully before buying. If it's a tube amp, have a tech check the condition of the tubes. Are they on their last legs? Remove the speaker grille and look at the cones. Are they ripped? Are they pushed in? With the amp on, and the volume up, turn the knobs back and forth. If they're a bit scratchy, you can clear them with a squirt of spray cleaner. Finally, leave the amp on for a while. Sometimes it won't act up until it's hot.

In the hands of a skilled technician, a used amp can be made even better than new. Proper maintenance and refurbishing can work wonders for an old tube amp, but the cost of an extensive refurb can be high.

MISTAKES

Some guitarists simply march into a music store, buy the amp their guitar hero uses, and then are surprised they can't get the same sound. They forget that studios often use lots of expensive rack gear to process the recorded sound. Because the acoustics are different, amps never sound the same at home as they do in the store.

Neglecting your homework also leads to problems. Some buyers won't look at a brand or model they're not familiar with. Suppose you're shopping for a practice amp, and a difference of only $10 or $15 might get you several additional features, such as a line-out jack, a headphone jack, and better EQ. If you don't do the research, you'll lose. Try to keep an open mind when auditioning unfamiliar brands and products. Trust your years.

Also, a lot of people make the mistake of thinking you can't get a big amp sound from a small amp, but if it's a quality device, you often can. In extreme cases, there are people buying huge back-breaking stacks just because they look good, not because they're what's needed. Many of these rigs may never leave the basement.

CURRENT TRENDS

The last few years have seen dramatic advances in digital signal processing (DSP). There are many amps today that offer a multitude of impressive built-in digital effects. Software-based modeling amps are on the cutting edge of a new technology that can provide a breathtaking variety of impressive tones that emulate the classic amps of the past while also providing dramatic new sounds for the future. The leading amp builders today are offering amps with more versatility than was previously imaginable. Amp modeling technology is still in its infancy; the future is sure to hold more amazing advances. ∎

A GLOSSARY OF AMPLIFIER TERMS

The definitions here are presented in a music-related context rather than in technical terms, to help you clarify the jargon found in manufacturers' brochures and operators' manuals.

We've included definitions of terms in such diverse areas as electrical phenomena and concepts, as well as amplifier hardware. Cross-referenced words are in bold type.

AC (alternating current). Electric current that reverses its direction (alternates) at regularly occurring intervals. In North America, power from a standard wall socket is 120 volts AC, alternating at 60 cycles per second. Audio signals in amps, effects, wires, etc., are also AC. See **DC**.

AC outlet. Frequently referred to as a convenience or courtesy outlet (usually found on the back of an amp), this feature provides an extra socket for powering auxiliary equipment.

Active. Pertaining to electronic circuits (such as tone controls) that add to as well as subtract from a given signal. Such circuits often require power sources. See **Passive**.

Active tone controls. Tone controls that add to and attenuate, rather than just cut from, an audio signal.

Amperes (amps). The unit of measurement used to represent electrical **current** flow and its density.

Amplifier (amp). An electronic device that increases the level of an audio signal, usually for the purpose of driving one or more speakers, or for maintaining proper levels in long signal chains (multiple effects, long cords, etc.).

Attenuate. To reduce the **voltage**, **power**, or frequency of a signal.

Balanced connector. A three-conductor connector—commonly referred to as an XLR or Cannon connector—that terminates a cord carrying a signal over three wires. One wire acts as a ground, while the others carry the signal in the form of positive and negative **voltages**.

Bass control. A tone control that affects low audio frequencies (typically below 500 Hz).

Biasing. The process of adjusting an output **tube's** idle **current**. Proper biasing increases reliability and tube longevity.

Bright switch. A feature that emphasizes an **amp's** high frequencies.

Capacitor. An electronic component that blocks **DC**, but allows **AC** to pass. Capacitors are commonly used in tone-control and **power**-supply circuits.

Channel. An individual **preamp** section, usually with independent **volume** and tone controls. Many **amps** provide multiple channels for more flexibility.

Channel switching. A feature that allows an audio signal to be routed from one channel to another, usually by means of a **footswitch**.

Chassis. The sheet-metal frame to which electronic components (**capacitors**, **resistors**, etc.) are mounted.

Circuit breaker. A device found on the backs of some amplifiers that automatically interrupts a circuit carrying potentially damaging **current**; often used instead of a **fuse**.

Combo amp. A cabinet that houses both an **amplifier** and speakers.

Compression. A feature of some **amps** and effects that reduces the signal's **dynamic range** by making loud sounds quieter and quiet sounds louder. See **Limiter**.

Current. The flow of electricity through a circuit. See **Amperes**.

dB (decibel). A unit of measurement for expressing the ratios of various quantities including sound level, **power**, and **voltage**. Basically, decibels represent degrees of relative loudness, on a scale starting from zero for the least perceptible sounds. Prolonged exposure to levels of more than 90–95 dB can cause permanent hearing damage; amplified rock music averages about 120 dB at a distance of 4–6'. For more on hearing loss and hearing protection, check www.hearnet.com.

DC (direct current). Electric **current** that has constant and uniform polarity (flows in

one direction). Batteries and small power sources for effects provide a source for **DC**. See **AC**.

Depth. A general term often used in describing the intensity of an effect such as **reverb**, phasing, etc.

Direct out. A balanced **output** that uses XLR plugs to send a signal to a recording console or PA mixer.

Distortion. Also referred to as clipping, distortion is a change in an audio signal resulting in the appearance of frequencies at the **output** that were not present in the original waveform. Distortion commonly results from a signal that is too powerful to be adequately handled by an **amp**, speaker, or other electronic device. Guitarists often use distortion to create **sustain**.

Distortion effect. A feature that intentionally causes an **amp** to sound overdriven.

Dynamic range. The difference between the minimum and maximum (overload) signal level in audio equipment. Often measured in **decibels**.

Effects channel. A **channel** that includes an effects device (phaser, **distortion**, flanger, etc.). See **Phase**.

Effects loop. Often composed of an **output** jack and an **input** jack that allow you to connect effects between an **amplifier's** preamp and the **power amp** (or a successive **preamp**). Because the signal level from a preamp is much higher than that from most guitars, the signal-to-noise ratio can be greatly increased by using an effect between **amp** stages rather than between the instrument and the amp.

EQ (equalization). The intentional altering of portions of the audio frequency spectrum by means of **filters** or tone controls; often employed to reduce uneven **frequency response** or feedback.

Extension speaker jack. A feature usually found on the back of an amp that allows a remote speaker to be used.

FET (field-effect transistor). A kind of **solid-state** device that is often more stable than standard transistors.

FET distortion. When overdriven, a **FET** exhibits **distortion** qualities more like that produced by a **tube** than by most other types of transistors.

FET switching. Circuits containing **FETs,** which can be used to activate effects or perform **channel-switching** functions with low noise and low **power** consumption.

Filter. An electronic tone control circuit that alters certain frequencies.

Footswitch. A foot-triggered switch used to activate an **amp's reverb, vibrato,** or other feature, as well as effects devices.

Frequency response. The range of frequencies over which a device or audio system will perform.

Fuse. A replaceable protective device that breaks a circuit when the **current** becomes abnormally high. A fast-blow fuse is generally used in delicate circuits, whereas a slow-blow fuse is used in more rugged ones. See **Circuit breaker.**

Fuse holder. A socket or metal clip that allows for easy replacement of a **fuse.** Generally located on the back of an **amp** or within the **chassis.**

Gain. The amount an **amplifier** increases the **power** of a signal, usually expressed in **decibels.** See **Volume.**

Graphic equalizer. A device containing multiple **filters** with separate, fixed frequency centers, which allows for the boosting or cutting of particular signal ranges. See **Parametric equalizer.**

Ground (also called "earth"). The electrically neutral part of a circuit, often referred to in terms of 0 volts.

Ground switch. Also referred to as a line-reverse or polarity switch, this feature allows the polarity of the **AC** line to be quickly reversed, resulting in reduced hum.

Headroom. Expresses the relative difference between the operating and maximum operating points of an audio device.

Heat sink. A metal device with surface areas maximized to dissipate the heat electronic components generate.

Hertz (Hz). A unit equal to one cycle per second that measures the frequency of a periodic phenomenon such as an **alternating current.**

Hiss. A kind of undesirable audio frequency noise. Often called white, pink, or thermal noise.

IC (integrated circuit). Also known as a "chip," an IC is a highly miniaturized **solid-state** circuit that contains the equivalent of many components such as transistors, **resistors, capacitors,** diodes, etc.

Impedance. Measured in **ohms,** impedance is the total opposition to the flow of **alternating current** in a circuit. Impedance is an important factor in pairing a speaker and an **amplifier.** See **Matching impedance.**

Inputs. The entry points where the signal from a guitar or effect may be introduced to an **amplifier** or other electronic device.

LED (light-emitting diode). A small light commonly used to indicate various **amp** functions.

Limiter. An electronic circuit that acts much like a compressor, except that it keeps a signal's **dynamic range** within fixed limits.

Master volume. Simultaneously controls the overall volume of one or more **channels** of an **amp.** When used in conjunction with a **channel's volume** control, a master volume lets you control the amount of **distortion** as well as the overall output of the **amp.**

Matched tubes. Vacuum **tubes** selected for their similar electrical characteristics. Often employed in **amps** to produce more efficient operation.

Matching impedance. When the output **impedance** of a device (such as an **amplifier**) is compatible with the input impedance of a device (such as a speaker) to which it is connected, the two are said to match. Mismatched impedances can lead to **distortion,** signal loss, poor **frequency response,** or even blown **amps.**

Midrange control. A tone control that affects audio frequencies in the middle range, where the largest concentration of audio energy is usually present.

Modeling. A software-based process that can produce a wide variety of **amp** tones and effects textures.

Noise floor. The level at which noise (hiss, hum, etc.) exists in an **amplifier.** Often used as a reference point in signal-to-noise ratios.

Ohm. Represented by the Greek letter omega (Ω), an ohm is the unit used to measure electrical resistance or **impedance.**

Outputs. Jacks normally located on the back of an **amp** that allow you to attach one or more auxiliary speakers.

Overdrive level. The level at which **distortion** begins as a consequence of feeding a device with an overloading signal.

Overload. A load that exceeds an **amplifier's** capability.

Parametric equalizer. An equalizer with one or more center frequencies that are variable over a particular range, in addition to boost and cut capabilities. See **Graphic equalizer, EQ.**

Passive. Pertaining to electronic circuits that generally subtract from a signal and which require no power source. See **Active.**

Passive tone controls. Tone controls that only attenuate, or cut from, an audio signal. Generally a simple circuit, such as a **potentiometer** and a **capacitor,** requiring no external power. See **Active tone controls.**

Peak wattage. Also referred to as peak power, peak wattage is a signal's maximum instantaneous **power. Amplifiers** are able to perform at their peak for only short periods of time. See **RMS.**

Phase. The alignment between two soundwaves. Waves of the same frequency and amplitude that are aligned from peak to trough are in phase. Certain sonic effects are produced by alterations in phase.

Piggyback. An **amp** and speaker-cabinet combination in which the head (amp

A GLOSSARY OF AMPLIFIER TERMS

circuitry) and speakers are each housed in their own enclosures.

Pilot lamp. A light that indicates whether an **amp** or other electrical device is turned on.

Potentiometer (pot). A variable resistor used for an amplifier's volume and tone controls.

Power. Working electrical energy measured in watts. See **Wattage**.

Power amp. An **amplifier** that has higher power-output capability than a **preamp** and is designed to drive one or more speakers. Generally contained with the preamp in self-contained or **piggyback** amps, but also sometimes available as a separate unit.

Power amp in. An input that plugs directly into an amp's **power amplifier** and bypasses the **preamp**. This function allows an **amp** to be used as a **slave**.

Power supply. Coverts the **AC** line **voltage** into the various **DC** voltages the amp's circuitry requires.

Power rating. The maximum **power** at which an **amplifier** can operate over a specified period.

Preamp. An **amplifier** stage that raises the signal of a low-level source (such as a guitar) so that it may be further processed.

Preamp out. An **output** that lets you take the **preamp's** signal and send it to other **power amps**, PA mixers, or recording gear.

Presence. A control that boosts frequencies above the range of the **treble control**.

Push-pull switch. A switch that you operate by a pulling or pushing movement; often combined with a **potentiometer**.

Rectifier. An essential component of an amp's **power supply**, a rectifier converts **AC voltage** into the **DC** voltage the **amp's preamp** and **power amp** circuitry requires. Tube rectifiers provide more dynamic voltage **sag** than **solid-state** rectifiers.

Resistance. The opposition to **current** flow, expressed in **ohms**.

Resistor. A component possessing primarily the property of resistance. See **Ohm.**

Reverb. The synthetic creation of spatial ambience, or reverberation—echoes spaced so closely together they aren't discernible as individual events. Reverb is most commonly produced by sending a signal through an electronic delay device. Guitar **amps** have traditionally used a module (or "tank") containing metal springs to provide the delay. Some amps use digital signal processing (DSP) to produce reverb.

RMS (root mean square). The most meaningful measure of an amp's **power**, RMS is based on continuous power at a given number of cycles per second over a period of time of no less than 30 seconds. See Peak **wattage**.

Sag. A lowering of **power** supply **voltage** as output power demands increase. **Power supply** sag creates a compressor-like dynamic effect.

Slave. A **power amplifier** that is driven by the **preamp** of another **amp**. Slave amps are often used to provide extra **power** to drive additional speakers.

Solid state. Refers to electronic components such as diodes and transistors that use semiconductors (crystals) instead of **tubes**.

Speaker emulator. Tone-shaping circuitry that mimics a guitar speaker's limited **frequency response**. Speaker emulators are commonly used when recording direct.

Standby switch. A feature that allows **tubes** to idle (remain warm) while an amp is not in use, such as between sets. This reduces the strain on tubes that frequent heating and cooling causes.

Sustain. The phenomenon in which a sound such as a note or chord continues without appreciable degradation or decay.

Toggle switch. A two- or three-position switch operated by flipping (toggling) a protruding lever.

Top (head). An amplifier unit that is separate from any type of speaker enclosure.

Transformer. Commonly a large, square, or toroidal (doughnut-shaped) component used in an **amp's power supply** to convert **AC** main **voltage** to other suitable AC voltages. Transformers sometimes are used as as buffers between amps and speakers in order to match their **impedances**.

Transient response. The ability of an **amplifier** to handle sudden changes in audio levels without **distortion**.

Treble boost. Electronic augmentation of high-frequency signals.

Treble control. A tone control that affects high frequencies (typically above 5000 Hz).

Tremolo. An effect feature on many amps, tremolo is the variance in the amplitude (**volume**) of a sound—generally at a rate of between .5 and 20 times per second—achieved by the use of a low-frequency oscillator. Commonly mistakenly referred to as **vibrato**.

Tube. Also referred to as a vacuum tube or valve, a tube is a sealed glass envelope in which the conduction of electrons takes place through a gas or vacuum, most often for amplification or switching applications.

Vibrato. An effect feature that uses an oscillator to cause a regular variation in the frequency (pitch) of a sound. **Amps** that have this feature usually have speed and intensity controls for governing the velocity and **depth** of the vibrato effect.

Voltage. Electrical pressure that causes **current** to flow through a conductor. Its unit of measurement is the volt.

Volume. The overall amount of loudness. See **Gain**.

Wattage. The output **power** capability of an **amplifier**. See **Peak wattage, RMS.** ∎

ABOUT THE AUTHORS

Jesse Gress is author of Backbeat's *The Guitar Cookbook* and is *Guitar Player* magazine's music editor. Jesse tours and records with Todd Rundgren and the Tony Levin Band.

Terry Buddingh is a factory-authorized service tech for major amp manufacturers and a Contributing Technical Editor for *Bass Player* magazine. He has also served as amp tech for artists such as Green Day and Third Eye Blind.

Richard Johnston is Backbeat Books' executive editor and a former editor of *Guitar Player, How To Play Guitar,* and *Bass Player* magazines.

Andy Ellis is editor of the recently revived *Frets* magazine and a consulting editor for *Guitar Player* magazine. He also originated the Sessions instructional series.

Arlen Roth is the author of 12 books, including *Hot Guitar,* a collection of his columns that appeared in *Guitar Player* for 10 years. He also founded the Hot Licks

audio/video instructional series (www.hotlicks.com). His latest album is *Drive It Home* [Solid Air].

Flatpicking pioneer **Dan Crary** is known for his interpretations of traditional guitar tunes. He's also a professor of speech and communication at California State University, Fullerton. His most recent recording is *Dan Crary & Lonnie Hoppers and Their American Band* [Pinecastle].

Guitarist, author, and teacher **Happy Traum** is a veteran performer and recording artist who runs the instructional-video company Homespun Tapes (www.homespuntapes.com).

Richard Gartner is a founding editor of Frets magazine and a founder of the Strawberry Music Festival.

Performer, arranger, author, and clinician **Howard Morgen** is on the faculty of the Guitar Study Center of the New School in Manhattan and the Jazz Studies Program of the C.W. Post Campus of Long Island University.

Tom Darter is the founding editor of *Keyboard* and an eminent composer, performer, and instructor.

Guitarist and arranger **John Carlini** has collaborated with such artists as bandleader David Grisman.

Dan Erlewine is Director of Technical Operations for Stewart-MacDonald Manufacturing and author of *The Guitar Player Repair Guide* and *How to Make Your Electric Guitar Play Great!* He also repairs guitars for many well-known players.

Johnny Smith was a valuable contributor to *Guitar Player* for many years. He won numerous polls as a jazz soloist and became the namesake for one of Gibson's elegant archtop guitars.

Ed Schilling has contributed many articles to *Guitar Player* through the years.

NOTES

NOTES

NOTES

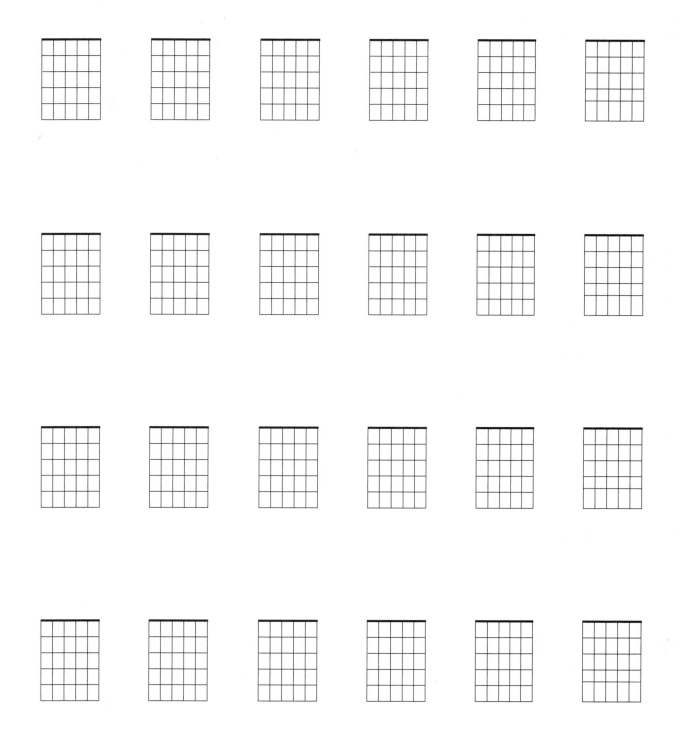

NOTES

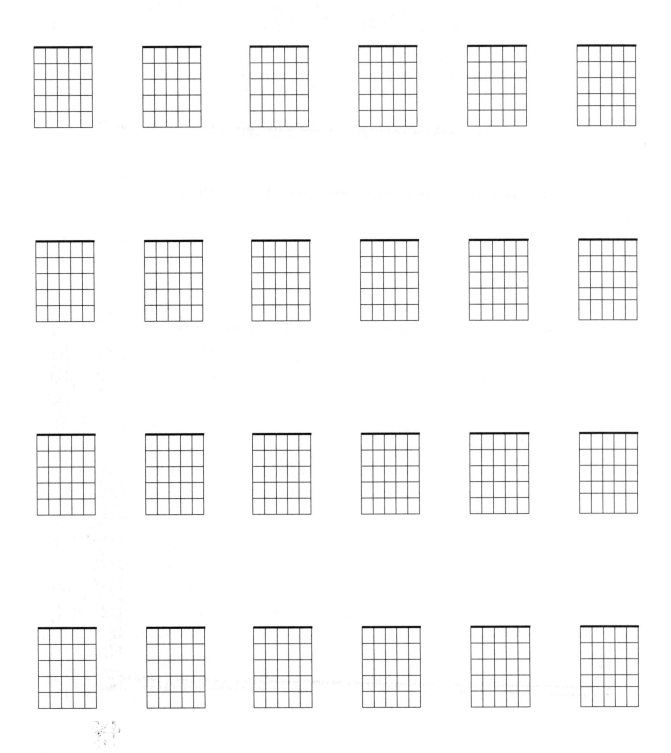

Serious Players.

The Music Player Network is for serious players. From guitars, bass, keyboards and recording to computer music culture, dance, trance and more. • Our industry-leading magazines, *Guitar Player*, *Keyboard*, *Bass Player*, *Gig*, *MC²*, *Rumble*, *EQ* and *Extreme Groove*, take the art of playing music seriously. And so does our leading portal website, MusicPlayer.com. • Our editors and writers are experienced musicians and engineers with special insights and hands-on experience that only comes from real-time playing. • If you want to get serious about your playing, check us out at your nearest newsstand or visit MusicPlayer.com on the web.

MPN
MUSIC PLAYER NETWORK

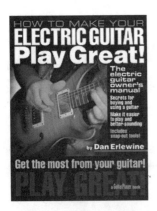
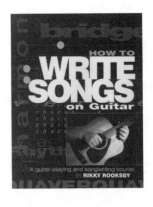
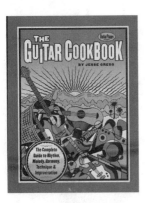

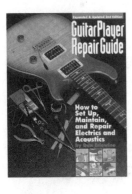